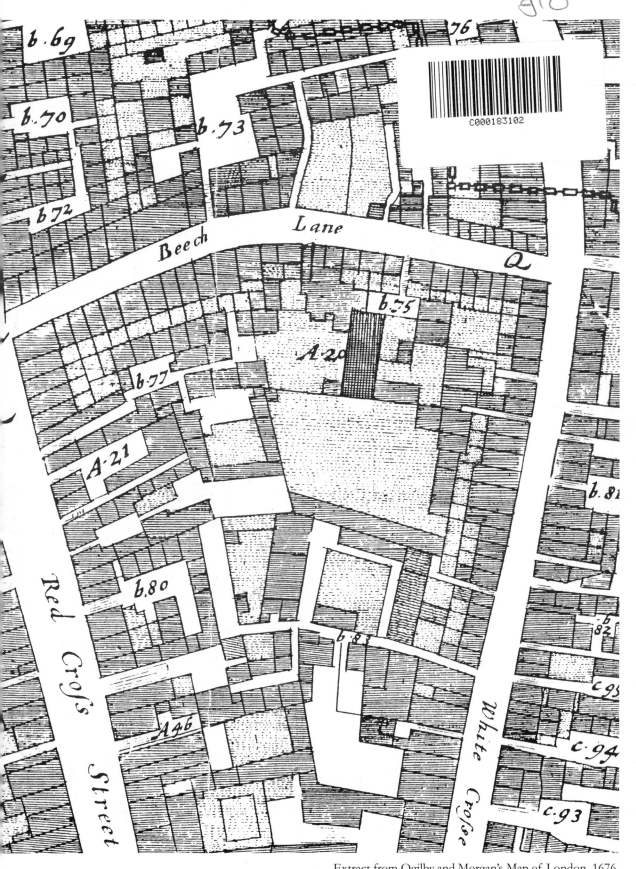

Extract from Ogilby and Morgan's Map of London, 1676.

A HISTORY OF

THE WORSHIPFUL COMPANY OF GLOVERS
OF LONDON

Sir Christopher Collett, GBE, Lord Mayor 1989, Master of the Company of Glovers 1981-2

A HISTORY OF

THE WORSHIPFUL COMPANY OF GLOVERS
OF LONDON

Ralph W. Waggett

Phillimore

2000

Published by
PHILLIMORE & CO. LTD.
Shopwyke Manor Barn, Chichester, West Sussex

ISBN 1 86077 123 8

Printed and bound in Great Britain by
BOOKCRAFT LTD.
Midsomer Norton

Contents

Foreword

RALPH WAGGETT approached me during my last week as Master of the Glovers Company, in November 1993, with a proposal to research and write a detailed history of the Glovers for publication in time for the millennium in A.D. 2000. Ralph had served the resuscitated Fellmongers of Richmond, Yorkshire as its first Master and subsequently as Clerk, where he had shown his propensity for detailed research. Knowing this, I replied that he would receive my whole-hearted support for this project. We agreed at that time that the writing of the history would not be made public knowledge until he had produced a first draft and then, at that time, I would commend it to the Court of the Glovers Company for approval, which I did in 1997.

An earlier brief history of the Company has been written by Liveryman Peter Lawson-Clarke in 1982, which gave an excellent overview of the Company's activities. We felt, however, that a definitive history was appropriate to mark the 650 years that have passed since the publication of our first known archives in 1349 and that this should span the years up to the 350th anniversary celebration of our current Charter obtained from Charles I in 1638.

This history is a serious work, but despite its wealth of factual detail, anyone interested in the rich history of our country and, in particular, the story of the 'wax and wane' of our glove manufacturing craft over the centuries, should find Ralph's history a fascinating source of information. I admire him for the enormous amount of research and scholarly effort he has lovingly given to write this book and wish to thank him, on behalf of all his fellow Glovers and those involved with the glove industry of Great Britain, for his efforts, which, after six years, have now come to fruition.

JOHN WOOD
Master 1992-3

List of Illustrations

Acknowledgements

I N WRITING THIS BOOK I have had no end of help and it is as much a pleasure as a duty to acknowledge the fact.

The Epilogue is largely based on information supplied to me by Past Masters Sir Christopher Collett and Barry St John Reed. Sir Christopher compiled a full account of the conditions leading to the reforms of the 1970s and the action then taken and Mr. Barry Reed kindly supplied me with various notes and memoranda compiled from that time in his possession.

Past Master Fred Caine has made numerous suggestions and his knowledgeable comments have invariably proved helpful.

Latterly I have had two notable 'research assistants'. Our present Master, Mrs. Margaret Linton, has been smitten with the desire to carry out research into the history of the Company. Perhaps she will go on to make new discoveries. First Under Warden Alan Howarth's love of the City is known to all who have read his occasional articles in *The Glover* and he has been helpful in investigating the Company's 18th-century Lord Mayors.

There are two other liverymen to whom I am particularly indebted. The Renter Warden, Jim Clarke, took me in hand and guided me with good sense and good humour along the path leading to publication. Past Master John Wood is the Chairman of the Company's Archives Committee. He has been a constant support and inspiration and has given me constant encouragement. Without his aid and advice this history would not have been produced.

Over and beyond my debt to my fellow liverymen I owe my thanks to many others.

The Master, Wardens and Court of Assistants of the Worshipful Company of Leathersellers kindly made their Court minutes for the first half of the 17th century available to me for study. Without that generous gesture it would have been impossible for me to attempt to give a balanced account of the Glovers' struggle for independence.

Mr. Roy Thomson, BSc, C.Chem, FRSC, FSLTC, Chief Executive of The Leather Conservation Centre, Northampton, has allowed me to quote from his authoritative 'Leather manufacture in the post-medieval period with special reference to Northamptonshire' and 'Leather Manufacture through the Ages'.

Barbara Allen, the Honorary Secretary of the Cripplegate Ward Club, was both charming and helpful in dealing with my enquiries and Mr. Wilfred Dewhirst willingly permitted me to make reference to the information contained in 'The Ward of Cripplegate in the City of London' of which he is joint author.

I am most grateful to Dr. I.G. Doolittle for allowing me to quote extensively from *The City of London and its Livery Companies*, to Dr. E. Dorothy Graham, General Secretary of the Wesley Historical Society, for giving me permission to include excerpts from John

Wesley's *Journal* and to the British Library for granting leave to use the Lansdowne and Additional Manuscript collections.

I have received the most generous help from the City Archivist who has permitted me to take quotations from the Repertories of the Court of Aldermen, the Journals of the Court of Common Council and the documents held in the Companies Box, *My Lord Mayor* by Valerie Hope, and *The Corporation of London: its origins, constitutions, powers and duties* by P.E. Jones.

The Keeper of Prints and Maps at Guildhall Library has kindly allowed me to make ample reference to the contents of Sir John Baddeley's *Cripplegate, one of the Twenty Six Wards of the City of London* and to reproduce part of Ogilby and Morgan's map of the City and to include portraits of three eminent Glovers.

I am indebted to Penelope Ruddock, Curator of the Museum of Costume in Bath, for permission to reproduce a number of photographs of gloves taken from the collections of the Worshipful Company of Glovers of London on loan to the Museum of Costume, Bath.

Finally, I would like to express my gratitude to Mrs. Joyce Hutchinson, my most patient and loyal ally and amanuensis, who has by her efforts enabled this work to go to publication, and to my fellow liveryman Miss Pat Winterton, the transcriber of one of the Company's minute books for the period 1675-9, and especially to Peter Lawson-Clarke whose *Brief History of the Company* is a mine of useful information and whetted my appetite to delve deeper into the history of the Company.

RALPH WAGGETT

November 1999

Preface

L IKE ANCIENT GAUL, the history of the Glovers' Company may be divided into three parts. First there was the period from the establishment of the Company or its possible predecessor, the Fraternity of Glovers, probably during the 14th century until its amalgamation, initially in 1498, with the Company of Pursers and then, in 1502, with the Leathersellers' Company. The second period covers the time when the Company ceased to have an independent existence and was subsumed within the ranks of the more powerful Company of Leathersellers. That continued until 1638. The third and last period began with the re-emergence of the Glovers as a separate Company and continues to the present day.

After a long struggle to regain its independence the Company of Glovers was granted its Charter by the Crown in 1638. It succeeded in having its ordinances or bye-laws accepted and enrolled by the Court of Aldermen in 1644 and in 1680 it had its status confirmed as a livery company.

Sadly, although it is one of the most ancient of the livery companies, comparatively few of its records now survive and much of its history is now lost to view. The very names of many Past Masters are unknown. The site of its livery hall has disappeared under the concrete of the modern Barbican development and in the last century the Company came near to extinction, this time through apathy and neglect. Now it is a thriving, lively society standing well in the forefront of livery activity, fulfilling its obligations to the City, to the gloving industry and to society through charitable activities. Its future seems assured in the hands of an active and interested membership of both men and women. Here I have made an attempt to look back as the Company stands on the threshold of a new century and to give an account of the vicissitudes through which this most enduring of societies has passed in the chances and changes of time.

The Glovers' skins are not tanned but allum'd; called often allum leather. He makes gloves of sheep, kid and doe skins and breeches of shamy (sheep skin differently dressed from the other) and buck skin. Often the glover and breeches maker are the same trade. Glover lines gloves with furs and rabbit skins and sometimes sells muffs and tippets of fur and ermine. Chief instruments (like a taylor) are sheers and needle. Not many hands employed in London and many are women. The Glover cuts them into their several sizes and gives them cut to be served at so much a pair. A good hand earns 10s. or 12s. per week. The shops are mostly supplied from the country. This art requires neither much strength nor ingenuity – a sedentary stooping business, it disagrees with a consumptive or physicky disposition.

R. Campbell, *The London Tradesman*, 1747

The glovers and gloves of England excell all those of any other Nation whatsoever which is the cause great quantities are exported yet the art is more opprest than any other trade of the Kingdome for want of a government.

The Glovers petition for a Charter 1637 [SP.16/386]

A Fraternity and Craft

REFERENCES TO INDIVIDUAL GLOVERS first appear in the 14th century and they are fairly frequent. The Letter Books of the Corporation of London mention Thomas le Glover,[1] who, in 1318, was required to find, i.e. provide, a foot soldier for King Edward II. In 1387 Henry le Glover[2] appears in a list of archers sent to parts of Gascony by the Mayor Aldermen and Commonalty of London in aid of the King's war with the King of France. Henry le Glover called 'le Fanere'[3] (perhaps the same Henry) had to contribute £10 towards a loan of £5,000 to the King. In 1345 Robert le Glover[4] was a juryman and there are other similar references to glovers appearing during the remainder of the century.

On 12 March 1350 it is recorded[5] that many false gloves and *braels* (belts) were burnt in Chepe. The record shows that

> on Monday next after the Feast of St Gregory the Pope in the 24th year of the reign of King Edward III the men of the trade of Glovers who had been sworn to keep the Articles of the trade, came and brought before Walter Turk, Mayor, and the Aldermen 17 pairs of gloves found upon John Francies of Northampton. The said men of the trade of Glovers brought also 28 braels called bregirdles (belts or girdles) found upon divers men (named) asserting that the said gloves and braels were of false fashion and vamped up of false materials in deceit of all the people and to the scandal of the whole trade … Therefore it was awarded that the said gloves and braels should be burnt in the high street of Chepe near the Stone Cross there and accordingly on the same Monday they were burnt according to the award aforesaid.

In 1372 the Chamberlain received from various misteries[6] a present for the King. The Glovers gave 20 shillings.[7] However, in 1376 a list of 48 companies providing Common Councillors did not include the Glovers.[8]

It is not now possible to say how or when glovers began to associate together as one body.[9] The burning of the gloves in Chepe took place in 1350 and the quotation from Riley refers to the 'Articles of that trade'. This must refer to the ordinances or bye-laws of the Company made the year before which show a degree of organisation allowing the Company

---

[1] R.R. Sharpe, *Calendar of Letter Books of the Corporation of the City of London* (London, 1899-1912), Letter Book E, p.94. (Hereafter Sharpe, *Calendar of Letter Books*).   [2] Sharpe, *Calendar of Letter Books*, Letter Book F, p.12.
[3] ibid., p.47.   [4] ibid., p.262.
[5] H.T. Riley, *Memorial of London and London Life* (London, 1868), p.245.
[6] From the French 'mystere', a trade.
[7] Sharpe, *Calendar of Letter Books*, Letter Book G, p.172.
[8] W.H. Black, FSA, *History and Antiquities of the Worshipful Company of Leathersellers of the City of London* (London, 1871), p.18. (Hereafter Black, *History of Leathersellers*).
[9] According to S. William Beck, in his *Gloves, their Annals and Associations* (London, 1883), the first mention of a Company of Glovers in England is in one of the miracle plays performed in 1327 at Chester. He quotes Harleian MS2013 for saying the Glovers performed 'The Blind Man and Lazarus'.

to be recognised as a coherent and responsible mistery. These ordinances are set out in an Appendix[10] to this book. They would be drawn up by, or on behalf of, the members themselves but from very early days they were subject to the approval of the City authorities. A statute of 1437[11] expressly provided that all ordinances made by companies must be approved and recorded by the chief governors of the City. The Glovers' ordinances are in the common form. They deal with the election of Wardens to govern the Company and they regulate apprenticeships, prohibit night work, provide for search by the Wardens, govern the grant of the freedom and provide that none but freemen shall use the trade. They also provide a forum for the government of their craft through their common interest. In its earliest days the Company is sometimes described as a trade or mistery and sometimes as a guild or fraternity. These terms impart different meanings. Guild or gild is of ancient origin and is derived from the word 'gilden', to pay. In other words it implied the presence of a common box to which members paid their contributions. A fraternity is a brotherhood, often or usually a brotherhood with religious and social connotations. Unwin shows that in medieval times the gild or fraternity was often the forerunner of the mistery.[12] Sometimes they existed side by side each embracing men of the same trade and eventually they seem to have merged to form the prototypes of the livery companies we know today. Unwin points out that lay trading associations were unknown to and would be viewed with suspicion by the civic authorities but the medieval church would usually give support and protection to those groups showing charitable and religious aims.[13] For this reason many modern livery companies can trace their beginnings to a religious fraternity centred on a particular City church or monastery.[14] What seems to have happened was that a group of those practising the same trade would come together naturally, that their religious devotions and social activities would be practised together, that such devotions would originally be seen as their principal object open and permitted by society, that from this beginning matters of trade regulation came to be imported into their proceedings and over a period of time grew to have greater significance. In time, the words, fraternity, mistery, craft and guild came to be used as alternative descriptions of the same organisation.

In the case of the Glovers' Company it is interesting to see that in 1354, i.e. five years after the earlier bye-laws were recorded by the City authorities, the articles and ordinances of the Fraternity of the Craft of Glovers were recorded and acknowledged before the Commissary of London so that these provisions might be enforceable by the Church.[15] The Commissary was an ecclesiastical official appointed by the Bishop of London and offenders might be brought before his court. Following so soon after the earlier ordinances it seems to imply that a mistery of glovers and a fraternity of glovers may have existed contemporaneously. These ordinances also are set out in an Appendix[16] to this volume but there are several matters which deserve examination and comment.

---

[10] Appendix I and see Sharpe, *Calendar of Letter Books*, Letter Book F, p.200.   [11] 15 Henry VI c 6.
[12] G. Unwin, *The Gilds and Companies of London* (London, 1908), p.52. (Hereafter Unwin, *Gilds and Companies*).
[13] Unwin, *Gilds and Companies*, p.108.
[14] This fraternal origin was stressed by the livery companies in their evidence to the Commissioners charged with preparing a report on the City companies in 1882. Dr. I.G. Doolittle in his book *The City of London and its Livery Companies* (Dorchester, 1982), says, at p.97, 'they averred they were not now nor ever had been trade guilds but friendly societies established to provide fellowship and succour for their members. Their trading role was a later extraneous and temporary one.'
[15] Unwin, *Gilds and Companies*, p.108.   [16] See Appendix II and Guildhall Library MS Prowet f.196.

In the first place they represent a mixture, of part religious and part lay significance though the balance is weighed heavily towards matters of faith. Many years later when the Glovers' Company came to be joined to the Leathersellers' Company it was said by the historian of the Leathersellers that the Glovers were thought to be 'a very devout Company'.[17]

These articles are dedicated in the preamble to the 'Worshipe of the Holy and Hye Trinite fadir and sone and Holy Goost And in the Worshipe of the blessed and Glorious Virgyne Mary Moder of oure Lorde Godde Jhesu Crist.' Seventeen articles follow. They celebrate especially the Annunciation and the Assumption of the Blessed Virgin Mary the brethren meeting at the Chapel of Our Lady set in the 'New Chirchawe beside London'. Members are enjoined to pay 1s. 4d. each year to provide wax tapers in the Chapel and the relief of poor brethren; they are to be fined if they fail to pay their quarterage or fail to attend church on feast days or on the burial of a deceased member. Specifically, they must attend Placebo and Dirige,[18] the services of the dead and at mass in their livery. Those absent without just cause are to be fined. In every case half the fines imposed go into the Fraternity's poor box and half to 'the olde werke' of St Pauls. Poor members without sufficient means for burial but who have paid their dues are buried at the expense of the Fraternity. On feast days they dine together and then worship together. The Fraternity of the Craft of Glovers like other fraternities had a livery which members wore on solemn occasions. Some of the provisions apply particularly to craft regulation and some have a mixed connotation. For example, a requirement that members behave in a seemly manner refraining from slander and foul language and that they take care of and attend formal occasion in their livery might apply to a religious or a trade organisation. On the other hand some provisions such as that stipulating that any apprentice taking up his freedom before the Chamberlain must be accompanied by his master and the Master and Wardens of the Company is clearly a trade requirement.

Confirmation that there must have been separate craft and fraternity organisations at the time these ordinances were registered is provided by the article which says:

> Also it is ordeyned that he or they the which hath be(en) resceyved or shalbe resseyved here after into a brothir of the same Fraternite if it so hadde be(en) that he or they have ben or hadde ben of the Craft of Glovers of the forseid Cite of London paieth etc.

Similarly, a member of the Fraternity if he is of the Craft of Glovers and has been a paid up member of the Fraternity for seven years and yet has not goods enough to meet the cost of burial is to have the ceremony provided at the expense of the Fraternity. So it appears beyond doubt that the Fraternity of the Craft of Glovers was not synonymous with the Craft of Glovers.

Twenty-nine brethren of the Fraternity signed the articles.

The church of the Fraternity was the chapel dedicated to the Blessed Virgin Mary at Newchirchawe without Aldersgate. A plot of land there was purchased by Sir Walter Manny in 1349 to be a burial place outside the City walls for those who died of the plague. The

---

17 Black, *History of Leathersellers*, p.43.   18 The opening words of the Vespers and Matins respectively in the Office of the Dead.

land was bought from the Master of St Bartholomew's Hospital and was one of three burial grounds opened to meet the needs of London at the time of the Black Death. It contained 13 acres and one rood and was known as Spital Croft situate outside Aldersgate. Sir Walter erected a chapel there dedicated to the Blessed Virgin Mary. The next year Robert de Elsingg left money by his will to be devoted to the new work without Aldersgate commonly called Newchirchhawe.[19] So the chapel in the new churchyard was indeed very new when the Fraternity began to worship there. However, in 1361 the land was acquired from Sir Walter Manny for the erection of a house for the Carthusians and by 1382, at least, the Carthusians were living there in what became known as the Charterhouse.[20] The chapel passed in 1611 into the hands of Thomas Sutton and has, of course, been altered and added to as the chapel of the hospital established since that time but perhaps parts of the original may still be preserved in the present building.

As well as having a chapel to worship in the Fraternity had a hall and there is a reference to the clerk of the craft. It would be nice to discover the location of the hall and the name of that early clerk but like so much else these facts are now unknown.

---

[19]   Henry A. Harbin, *A Dictionary of London* (London, 1918), p.430.
[20]   The Glovers subsequently worshipped at the Church of St Thomas of Acon (or Acre) in Cheapside.

II

Glovers, Pursers and Leathersellers Unite

I N VIEW OF the chequered relationship which seems to have bedevilled the Glovers and the Leathersellers Companies in later years it is worth noting that long before the Glovers were absorbed by the Leathersellers the two Companies were in dispute. The cause was one which was to crop up time and again for almost 200 years until the Companies finally resolved to go their separate ways. It concerned the right to search, i.e. examine, and approve skins used by glovers and to seal them so showing that they were satisfactory. What happened was that there was an overlapping or encroachment by members of one Company or the other and some liverymen would not obey the search of the Wardens of the craft to which they belonged.

On 30 March 1451 the two Companies jointly petitioned the Court of Aldermen for approval of a proposal to resolve their differences.[1] It was stated that the Leathersellers included many who used, made and sold points,[2] tawed leather[3] and other necessaries, and used the craft of glovers but would not submit to a search by the officers of the Glovers' Company. Similarly, there were Glovers using the leathersellers' trade and they would not submit to the Leathersellers' search. Many, glovers and leathersellers alike, working as members of other companies suffered no search at all.[4] The result was 'moche fals and disceivable workes unto the grete shame and reproef of all trewe werkers of bothe the same Craftes and grete hurt to the comonpeople and that often tymes grete grucchying discencion and debate amonge the werkers and sellers that beene of the same Craftes'. It was proposed that for the sake of unity and good accord four Wardens should be appointed each year (two from either Company) and sworn before the Lord Mayor to do their duty as searchers to the best of their cunning and power. They should then, accompanied by a Sergeant at Mace assigned to them by the Lord Mayor as a sign of his authority, carry out an even-handed and indifferent search of all those using the craft of glover or leatherseller. In the case of craftsmen belonging to other companies search was only to be made in the presence of a Warden of such company after due notice given. Those refusing to comply with the search were to be fined.

The Lord Mayor and Aldermen considering the proposals to be good, honest, reasonable and redounding to the public advantage 'decreed and sentenced' that they be allowed.

---

[1] Black, *History of Leathersellers*, p.30 and Sharpe, *Calendar of Letter Books*, Letter Book K, pp.334-5.
[2] Laces for fastening apparel, as, for example, attaching the hose to the doublet (where buttons would now be used).
[3] Leather of animals other than cattle processed using alum or oil.
[4] Because of the custom of London, for which see post and particularly Chapter IX. There was a caveat to those obtaining their freedom by redemption, however, in that the City normally required a bond or recognisance from the applicant that he would engage principally in the craft of the Company in which he was to become free. For a full discussion of the implications of this custom of London see R. Ashton, *The City and the Court 1603-1643* (Cambridge, 1979), pp.49, 50 and 58-61.

Already the diversity and flexibility of the custom of London is illustrated. By the 14th century the son of every freeman had the right to the freedom of his father even though he had never learned his father's trade. An apprentice, on completing his term, could take his freedom in his master's company, or, if he was the son of a freeman he could be free in his father's company. Once he was free he could trade as he wished and his own apprentices would have the same choices. For example, the City Letter Books show that in 1409[5] an apprentice was admitted to the Glovers' Company notwithstanding that he practised as a fishmonger. This flexibility, admirable in many ways and cherished by the City authorities, gave rise to problems as will be seen in the next chapter.

In 1464 the Company obtained a Grant of Arms from Garter King of Arms. The original grant has since been destroyed by fire.[6] An abstract of it was made at the time of the Herald's Visitation in 1634. It reads

> John Smert alias Garter principall herault and King of Armes Greetinges etc. It hath bene in all Regions kingdoms etc. and Chiefly in all notable Cities, that the brotherhoodes of Companies have used to have a Seale of Armes, being perticuler to the whole body thereof for the solemnizinge of any place or Act etc. And it is true that the honorable and wise persons Thomas Hoddesden and Nicholas Wright, Masters of the trade and Crafte of Glovers of London have shewed me, that this trade have, a parte by themselves, Maisters and other officers, Authorised to constitute make and putt amonge them Rules, and ordinances on the said trade a parte, for which cause needfull to have Armes to distinguish etc. And beinge nowe required by those Wardens aforesaid, I the said Garter have allowed given and graunted to the said Glovers of London and to their successors for ever, the Armes above in the marjent; by Pattent under my hand and Seale of my Armes dated the 20th of Octob(er) anno d(omin)i 1464.[7]

The Arms of the Glovers may be described as follows, on a field of six pieces of sable and argent, three rams salient argent armed and unguled or; and the crest is described as on a helm with a wreath argent and sable and mantlings gules doubled ermine a ram's head argent armed and issuing from a basket or filled with wool argent between two wings erect gules.[8] They were quartered with those of the Pursers and such quartered Arms were, after 1502, impaled with those of the Leathersellers. Many years later the Company of Leathersellers took steps to amend their Grant of Arms. The minutes[9] of the Company show that on 11 June 1631 the Company conferred with the College of Arms about altering the crest of a ram's head in a basket with wings which crest the court thought improper and 'rather an abuse to this Society than any worship or dignity'. On 16 July it was ordered that the King of Heralds draw a new patent replacing the present crest with a demy roe buck 'being the proper crest'.

---

[5] Sharpe, *Calendar of Letter Books*, Letter Book K, p.168.   [6] At Leathersellers' Hall in 1819.
[7] Black, *History of Leathersellers*, p.44.
[8] In April 1987 the Company obtained a Grant of Supporters from the College of Arms in which an apprentice and sempster dressed in appropriate clothing from the time of Charles I are represented. The Grant included the Company's motto, 'Warm Hands and True Hearts'. It is a curious fact that earlier this century the Company seems to have had a slightly different motto. Colonel Robert J. Blackham in his *London Livery Companies* refers to the Company's motto of 'Free Hearts and Warm Hands' and Mr. Leslie Pinkham, a past Master, in a booklet compiled for the National Association of Glove Manufacturers refers to the motto in identical words to those of Blackham. Blackham's book is not dated but internal evidence shows that it was written in the 1930s and Mr. Pinkham's account is dated 1947.
[9] Minute Book of the Leathersellers' Company 1623-32.

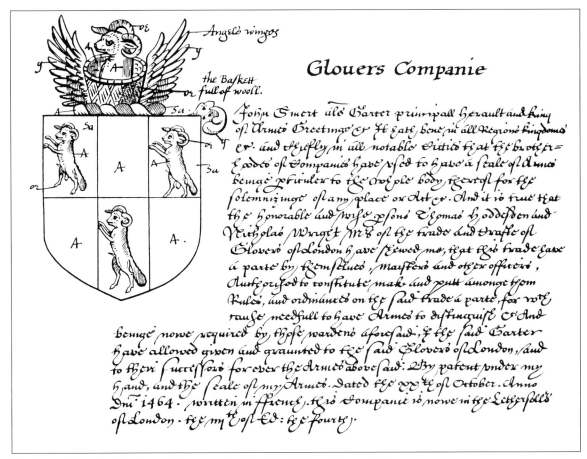

1   Grant of Arms by John Smert, Garter principal herald and King of Arms, 1464.

The proposal for a joint search by the two Companies does not seem to have resolved the matters of difference for long. The records of the Leathersellers' Company show that in 1479[10] 'we had much trouble and labor with the Pursers and also with the Glovers; and with much and great labor had of them our intent against them, according to the right. And also the Craft of Taweyears[11] came to us in the same year to be of the Craft of Leathersellers.'

On 15 October 1479[12] the Companies agreed to avoid dissention in relation to searches by making a new rule. Before the Court of Aldermen they agreed that each Company make search in its own mistery without the intervention of the other Company and that the Leathersellers should search in the Glovers Company in regard to those things pertaining to their mistery with the aid of a Sergeant at Mace and vice versa in the case of the Glovers.

10   Black, *History of Leathersellers*, p.37.
11   Usually described as whittawyers; those who tawed leather, an occupation inter-related to those of glover and leatherdresser.
12   Sharpe, *Calendar of Letter Books*, Letter Book L, p.168.

In 1482[13] the Glovers again petitioned the Court of Aldermen saying that they had become so impoverished 'and hindered sundry wises' by the influx of foreigners, i.e. countrymen, 'daily repairing to the Citee' and the lack of rules over them 'coming and working at their craft in the Citee' that they could not continue to bear the City's charges as they had hitherto done and asking that approval be given to certain rules set forth 'for the common wele of the Citee and the goode Rule of the said Craft'.

First they asked that an order be made that no freeman of the mistery or other person occupying the said craft should employ any foreigner until he had been admitted by the Wardens 'to be of habilite and conyng to exercise and use the same occupation', such foreigner first paying 6s. 8d. of which half should be paid to the Chamberlain and half to the Company's box. Then they said that such foreigner should be under the correction of the Wardens and sworn to keep the craft ordinances on pain of a fine divisible as before. Then they asked that it be ruled that no freeman of the mistery should teach anyone other than an apprentice or fellow freeman on pain of a fine and that none should take more than three apprentices at the most until they draw towards the end of their apprenticeship or else die.

The rules should further stipulate that no apprentice should be enticed from a fellow freeman; that wage-earners should be bound to the Wardens to pay 2d. for their quarterage; that freemen should not sell over any country gloves until they have been admitted by the Wardens to be 'well and lawfully made for the honour of the said Citee', and that every person of the craft should be ready to answer the summons of the Wardens 'for the honour of the Citee and the good rules and guiding of the craft'. All these rules were to be upheld by penalising offenders for any breach and the Glovers no doubt sought to facilitate their approval by agreeing that in each case half the fine should be paid to the Chamberlain. The petition was approved.

It does not seem that the lot of the Glovers' Company was much improved by this action. On 4 October 1498[14] they were again before the Court of Aldermen, this time making joint cause with the Pursers. Both Glovers and Pursers were users of tawed leather and so their economic requirements and abilities were no doubt similar. Sixty years before, a purser who nevertheless practised as a glover was admitted to that Company at the instance of the 'Masters and good men' of the Company and in 1443, conversely, a member of the Glovers' Company who practised as a pouchmaker was at the instance of the Pouchmakers, who were also workers in tawed leather, admitted to that Company.[15] Now the Glovers and Pursers joined together to petition for the union of their crafts. The petition begins with such a stately and eloquent preamble that it is here set out in full:

> In the name of Godde and of my blissed Seynt Mary the Virgin his glorious and blissed moder amen.
>
> For asmuche as amonges all thynges most plesant to my lord Godde in this transitory Worlde after due love had unto hym is the love Amyte and gode Accorde to be hadde amonges all Christian people And in esp[ec]iall amonges theym that be daily associate

---

[13] ibid., p.203, and see Corporation of London Records Office (hereafter CLRO) JOR 9 f.11.
[14] CLRO JOR 10 f.258 b.   [15] Sharpe, *Calendar of Letter Books*, Letter Book K, p.210.

togidere that like as their contynuell conv[er]sacion by reason of theyr dealyng must dayly be hadde and Accustomed So may they be knytte togidder in verrey true Amyte cheritably and kindely dealyng of the whiche groweth not onely such pleasure to Godde but Also the comon weell and prosp[er]ite of all theym that in suche wise deale. So always that their said dealyng be pute and sette under a due order Code and Ordinaire Rule.

No doubt that preamble became a standardised mantra in such cases. Unwin quotes it in another connection.[16] It is, however, an attractive and exemplary statement and its content can scarcely be improved upon.

The petitioners are then named: seven Pursers and six Glovers. It is recited that hitherto they have been able to pay their dues to the City 'having been ruled and kept in good order and many in number in metely substance' but now both fellowships are 'sore decayed' and cannot survive by themselves. They ask if they may join together as one company, made and named the craft of Gloverspursers and bound by their existing rules and ordinances with power to elect yearly four 'able and discreet persons' to be Wardens to govern the Fellowship. That petition was granted and so, from that date, for a time the Glovers' Company gave up its separate identity.

The union of the two companies proved to be no solution to their problems. Perhaps the small number of those signing the petition was an indication of their fragility. They seem to have realised quickly that the joint company had no stable future before it and on 7 June 1502, that is to say only about three and a half years after being joined together, the Gloverspursers having approached the Leathersellers' Company, that Company appeared before the Court of Aldermen to seek approval of certain terms to be agreed as a precondition to an amalgamation of the Companies.

---

[16] Unwin, *Gilds and Companies*, p.174.

III

The Union begins to Unravel

B Y THE TIME the Gloverspursers came to be absorbed within the Leathersellers' Company it had long become apparent that in economic terms a clear distinction must be made between the craft companies and the trading or mercantile companies. The concept of the craftsman buying his material direct from the producer, working on it and selling the finished product direct to the consumer had ceased to be a practicality within the City of London. A separation of functions had come into being. The capital needed to bring to the craftsman the sheep and lamb skins he required, often from distant parts of the kingdom or from Ireland, was provided by the merchant who similarly found a market for the finished product.

The craftsman was therefore doubly dependant upon the merchant who controlled both the price of the raw material and the price paid by the customer.[1] As time went on the disparity in wealth and influence between the merchant on the one hand and the craftsman on the other became more pronounced. The mercantile companies of London had, by 1502, become dominant. Already many had fine halls richly furnished, and their feasts and festivals attracted the support and attention of the nobility and even the Crown. On the other hand the craft company had little opportunity to expand its wealth and status and so could offer little by way of incentive to those who became its members. What it could offer was control of training, of workmanship and of quality of materials, but, as will be seen, even these requirements, which formed the very basis of the craft guild, became harder to meet.

In 1502, therefore, the situation of the Gloverspursers was very different from that of the Leathersellers' Company. The Leathersellers' was a trading company. Its senior liverymen were chiefly merchants trading in a variety of goods. Many had nothing to do with leather. There were, however, craftsmen as well. But just as there was a clear distinction between merchant and craftsman, so, by this time, there was also a well-defined distinction between those who aspired to the livery and those of lesser standing who did not – between the governors and the governed. This distinction, of course, applied in all companies but where membership of a company had a strong mercantile element richer and more influential than the rest it was this body which inevitably came to be the dominant group around whom the livery was based. In general terms it was a matter of wealth and standing which governed the position. Here the trader or merchant was at a clear advantage over the working craftsman. Those who did not succeed in acquiring the livery yet were freemen of the company fell into a category usually defined as yeomen, often with their own

---

[1] G. Unwin, *Industrial Organisation in the Sixteenth and Seventeenth Centuries* (London, 1904), p.107. (Hereafter Unwin, *Industrial*

officers, and so continued gradually declining in influence until their general decline into obsolescence in later years.[2]

The Gloverspursers were, therefore, in 1502 about to be absorbed into a company well able to face the hazards of the future and with a strong and secure presence in the City.

The proposals brought before the Court of Aldermen by the Company of Leathersellers were in the form of a bill or supplication. It listed a number of articles which the Gloverspursers required to be settled as a prior condition to an amalgamation. Black, in his *History of the Worshipful Company of Leathersellers of the City of London*, suggests that the union was attributable to the mediation of the Lord Mayor himself.

It is remarkable that the articles all related to matters appertaining to a guild or fellowship and not to matters of trade.[3] What they required was that the Fellowship should be under the patronage of the Virgin Mary of St Thomas of Acres[4] (now the Mercers' Chapel); that their common hall was to be dedicated to the Assumption and their dinner on the day of the Assumption. There is then a requirement which echoes the articles in the ordinances of the Fraternity of the Craft of Glovers registered before the Commissary of London 150 years earlier. The joint fellowship to be established should be

> partners in the suffrages done in the Charterhouse of London as the Gloverspursers then were and continue to maintain a light and hold a yearly obit there, with service for all the deceased Brethren and Sisters overnight and mass of Requiem on the morrow; that all the hangings of the Hall having any stories on them should be made of the stories of the blessed Lady and none of the Resurrection; likewise in the banner cloth with the Arms of the whole Fellowship to be set.

It is particularly interesting that the terms required to be agreed by the Gloverspursers related to the continuance of the practices so long observed by the Company. Although there had been great acrimony in the past (as there was to be in the future) about the search and seal of tawed leather, presumably the Gloverspursers thought that an amalgamation would take away the causes of dispute.

The bill or supplication was allowed by the Court of Aldermen and, for a time, there was peace. The Leathersellers' Company made a seal for its use bearing a representation of the Assumption and its Arms were impaled with those of the Gloverspursers.

A Deed Poll of 1509[5] setting out the ancient bye-laws of the Leathersellers' Company says

> Furthermore be it ordeyned that noo maner of persone occupying the trade of Leddersellers within the forsaide Citie or Franchise thereof make or doo to be made deceyvablie, or evell stuff, any gloves, that is to say of lambes ledder grayned of any maner of colour, of shepes ledder riband or frynged or bounde about with golde at the hand … upon payne every personne doeing contrarie to forfeite at every tyme to the use of the saide Fellowship xx[s] or more or lesse after the discrecion of the saide Wardeynes for the time being.

Organisation).
[2] Unwin, *Gilds and Companies*, p.343.
[3] Black, *History of Leathersellers*, pp.42-3. As he wryly comments, 'They are remarkable for dealing chiefly with religious observance of the Crafts, wherein the Gloverspursers seem to have been very zealous and punctilious.'

The Glovers remained vigorous and apparently increased greatly in numbers. However, towards the end of the 16th century both Glovers and Leathersellers were confronted by new problems arising.

At this time the Glovers Pursers and Poyntmakers (saying they represented those trades throughout the kingdom in that regard) petitioned the Privy Council[6] that an Act made in the first year of Queen Elizabeth's reign should be restored. This was an Act which prohibited the export of sheep skins and pelts unless they were staple ware. It benefited the home market and the Glovers and their allies alleged that it enabled them to buy sheepskins at fair prices. Sheepskins cost them 10s. per hundred and leather made of the same cost £1 for a hundred pieces. However, the Crown, hoping thereby to increase its revenues, had resorted to its dispensing power to set the Act aside. The result was to give a boost to exports and to drive up prices at home. Both pelts and leather had increased in cost greatly. Pelts now cost between 30s. and 5 nobles[7] per hundred and leather made of the same 50s. per hundred. As a result, the petitioners and indeed many other trades working in leather made of sheepskins[8] would have to discharge their workers and they and their children would be reduced to begging. It is a familiar story.

The petitioners pointed out that by statute

labouring men should only wear in their doublets canvas, fustian[9] or leather yet canvas for doublets costs 1s. 4d. an ell[10] and an ell and a half is required for a doublet; the worst fustian costs 1s. a yard and three yards are required for a doublet; three sheep skins of leather are needed for a doublet costing 2s. 8d. which a year last Christmas would have cost 1s. 4d.

Moreover, 'fustian and canvas are foreign goods and we have to spend our money abroad for them, whereas if leather was cheap labouring men would rather wear it because it lasts'. Because leather is dear a dozen good poynts cannot now (they say) be sold for 1d. as formerly 'and ordinary folk now wear threaden poynts made in Flanders to the ruin of English poyntmakers'. The whole country is affected. Almost every parish has a glover or poyntmaker. Some towns have twenty. Some cities have one hundred. The petitioners calculated that 2,000 people were maintained by these 'poor arts'.

It is a powerful plea but the Crown was not to be readily diverted and there was a long struggle which carried over into the next century before the sovereign's power to dispense with statutes was finally curbed.

About this date also a new danger arose and this time its effect was more widespread. The merchant leathersellers were themselves alarmed. For the purpose of improving her revenues and to enable her to reward her courtiers and favourites the Queen resorted to the granting of monopolies. In 1592[11] she granted to Mr. Edward Darcy by Letters Patent the right to regulate the view and search of leather of all kinds. All leather had to be examined by Darcy's agents and stamped or sealed on payment of a fee of 10d. a dozen

---

[4] See note 20, chapter I.   [5] Black, *History of Leathersellers*, p.45.
[6] British Library (hereafter BL) Lansdowne MS 114 Art 39.
[7] A former English gold coin first minted by Edward III having a then current value of 6s. 8d.
[8] 'The white tawyers, parchment makers, cofermakers, sadlers, bokebynders, bellowmakers, bowgetmakers, bruskmakers, case makers and shethers and letherdyers besides divers others arificers of this Realme.'
[9] Formerly a kind of coarse cloth made of cotton and flax, now a thick twilled cotton cloth with a short pile or nap.

for the lesser skins and as much as 10d. each for the better ones. The craftsman was to be bound in the very substantial sum of £40 not to deal in unstamped skins. The justification for this, as for other monopolies granted subsequently, was that it would remedy abuses in the existing system where the search by the companies themselves had fallen into desuetude. Much inferior leather came into the market and this would be eradicated by a new and efficient system.

The Leatherdressers and Glovers supported the grant to Darcy. For reasons described earlier they wished to obtain a better supply of material and they believed Darcy's patent would help them. On the other hand the Leathersellers opposed it as contrary to law and an unnecessary taxation of the common people, particularly the poorer sort who tended to wear leather.[12]

The companies concerned with leather had cause for alarm. Control of their commodity was being removed from them. Now the Leathersellers were joined by the Saddlers, the Girdlers, the Stationers and others. They complained to the Lord Mayor[13] about an order of the Privy Council requiring him to assist Mr. Darcy in regard to the patent the Queen had granted him. The fees to be paid to Mr. Darcy were calculated at 'an excessive and enormous rate' whereby the petitioners 'ar lyke utterlie to bee undoon'. They asked the Lord Mayor as Chief Governor of the City and also as principal Warden of the companies to use his best endeavours to get the patent suspended and their grievances reconsidered.

The Lord Mayor passed the petition to the Privy Council on 25 February 1592. He added his own comments that because the companies were both perplexed and troubled and felt that the patent would be the ruin especially of their poorer members he must ask the Privy Council to consider the complaints 'as to your grave wisdooms and discretions shall seem just'. To prevent a mass of individual petitioners troubling the Court directly he had urged them to be patient. The petition was not successful. In due course Mr. Darcy was to lose his monopoly but not before some of the principal Leathersellers had been imprisoned for their recalcitrance.

In 1593 the glovers and cutters of leather petitioned the Privy Council[14] concerning 'the miserable estate' of many thousands of such tradesmen throughout England and asked for reform of their 'lamentable greifes'. They alleged that the Leathersellers bought up all the leathers and skins in England, Ireland and Scotland that they could get hold of, whether good or bad. That had caused the price of white leather (used for making gloves) to rise from 20s. per hundred skins to 50s. or 60s. for the same number. They say that when the Leathersellers have bought many thousands of skins they pack them in dozens putting, say, four skins in each pack which are worth only a fraction of the value of the others. Yet (having bought the skins at varying prices reflecting their true worth) they sell them to the glovers at prices exceeding what they have paid for the very best skins. The glovers complain that they themselves are become discredited because their goods are in many instances made of bad skins. The Leathersellers gain by engrossing, i.e. buying up

[10] A measure of length, 45 inches.   [11] Unwin, *Gilds and Companies*, p.257.
[12] For an interesting description of the merits and qualities of tawed leather and its treatment see BL Lansdowne MS 74 Art 40 *et seq.* dealing with the Leathersellers' complaints against Mr. Darcy.
[13] BL Lansdowne MS 73 Art 17.   [14] BL Lansdowne MS 74 Art 50.

everything, and then by falsely packing bad skins among the good and that, say the glovers, is intolerable.

Those of the petitioners working within 30 or 40 miles of London were compelled to go to London to buy their leather, whereas but for the merchants engrossing the same they could buy locally better leather than they got from the merchants and at more reasonable rates and avoid the expense of travelling. Moreover, there were only about four individuals engrossing all the leather and they exported many thousands of skins; more than they had licence to do. The petitioners asked that someone be appointed to see that the export licence was adhered to and that a market be established at Leadenhall or elsewhere for the sale of white leather so that they could all go there on an equal basis to buy the skins the countrymen brought in. If the country suppliers were obliged to sell there the price of leather would come down and skins then being sold for 50s. and more per hundred would be reduced to 30s.

That is a highly significant complaint. It was to surface again in one form or another for the next 50 years until the Glovers regained their independence. It also reveals that the unity imposed by a company embracing such a wide variety of interests as glovers, leatherdressers, poyntmakers, pursemakers, fellmongers and whittawyers side by side with a dominating mercantile element was a fragmented creation. Such a sweeping allegation of bad faith, whether true or not, must have caused anger and resentment. Here we have the first stirrings of revolt by the Glovers.

IV

The Struggle for a Separate Identity

By THIS TIME the lack of homogeneity in the Leathersellers' Company had become pronounced. Its members had taken different sides in the dispute about Darcy's patent and the activities of the leather merchants. The craftsman worked often as part of a family unit or would employ a handful of journeymen or women to make gloves or poynts or purses from leather supplied to him and at prices set by his leatherseller colleagues who were, in effect, his employers. When he had made his gloves or purses the craftsman, who had no shop, tended to rely on the haberdashers to market them.

By this time, also, the workers in leather did not, in general, live and work within the City. They had moved south of the Thames to Southwark, Bermondsey and Lambeth. The reason was twofold. As long ago as the time of King Edward IV the main body of leatherdressers had been removed out of the City by public order as a sanitary precaution and there had been a migration of workers in leather to that area.[1] The other reason for the removal of leather workers was economic. The working craftsman could not afford to live and work within the City. He did not need a shop. The haberdasher provided an outlet for his goods and because his margin of profit was so tightly controlled by others who were more powerful he could not afford to live there either. By 1619[2] it was said that there were not above 40 members of the leather trades residing in the City while those in the suburbs numbered three thousand. So the disparity which existed already in the Company between the merchant trader on the one hand and the craftsman working at his handicraft on the other was underlined by the fact that most of those craftsmen did not even live and work near their colleagues and were inevitably under looser control of the Wardens. Moreover, on their part they felt less sense of belonging to the Company. Such a situation was bound to give rise to controversy and by 1611 or so the Glovers were already seeking their independence.

The Glovers were not alone. Their position was mirrored elsewhere. The situation was ripe for reform. Just as in earlier centuries the mercantile companies had absorbed many of the ancient craft guilds so the 17th century saw a loosening of the bonds and long before the century ended several were to regain, after long endeavour, their separate status. For example, the Feltmakers separated from the Haberdashers Company in 1604, and they were followed in the next year by the Pinmakers who became independent of the Girdlers' Company.[3]

There was no indication, however, of the struggle to come when, in 1612, the Leathersellers' Company petitioned the Court of Aldermen.[4] Their complaint was one

---

[1] By a charter of Edward III dated 6 March 1327 Southwark was granted to the citizens of London forever. P.E. Jones, *The Corporation of London – Its origins, constitution, powers and duties* (Oxford, 1950), p.178. (Hereafter Jones, *The Corporation of London*).
[2] Unwin, *Industrial Organisation*, p.128.   [3] Unwin, *Gilds and Companies*, p.263.   [4] CLRO Repertories (REP) 30.

which was to be frequently expressed. It concerned the influx of workers from the country districts which threatened to overwhelm the established tradesmen and destroy their ability to maintain good standards of workmanship. They pleaded that the trade of glovers was 'now greatly decayed, very few or none at all remaining that are freemen' of the Company. On the other hand,

> very great numbers of Forryners doe recide and dwell within and about the suburbes of this City exercysing the same trades and uttering deceiptfull wares without controlement so that noe reformacon of the abuses enseweth because there are not a convenient nomber of this Company using that trade to search and discover the manifold abuses in the cutting and making of gloves and purses.

They therefore humbly desired that they might have leave to admit 20 foreigners 'being working glovers' to assist the Company and thereby rectify the manifold abuses of the trade. The Court thought that was reasonable and it was allowed.

However, the number of 'foreigners' working in the suburbs must have continued to multiply considerably. Only seven years later the first positive steps against the governance of the Leathersellers' Company were taken. In 1619 the glovers and leatherdressers (whose trades overlapped) petitioned[5] Sir Julius Caesar, the Master of the Rolls, and the other members of the Privy Council, seeking permission to be incorporated as a separate company. They were to meet with, at best, indifference from the City authorities and hostility from the Leathersellers who were reluctant to concede any breakaway movement.

They began by saying that they numbered 3,000 souls and that for seven years they had been trying to become incorporated only for the good government of their craft. In stirring words which ring down the years they go on to say that they have twice received the Lord Chancellor's resolution that their petition was in order. Since then 'they are like the Israelites desiring to be delivered doubled in theire tasks, ye prices of theire materialls being enhanced to a great proporcion'. They humbly ask either to be incorporated 'whereby they are persuaded they shall passe the Red Sea of theire troubles from which they shalbe noe sooner delivered than they will sacrifice theire harteast thanks for your moste worthy honours and the reste of theire moste honourable benefactors. But if it be your honours' pleasure to send them back to theire Egyptians yet they humbly beseech your honours for a speedy resolution' that 'they may prepare theire neckes for the yoakes and theire hartes to the intollerable servitude they have heretofore endured.'

It was to be nearly 20 years before their prayers were successful but, nevertheless, from this time the struggle with the forces of opposition was joined.

The Leathersellers' reply was comprehensive.[6] There were seven grounds of objection to the petition. First of all they said there already was a corporation of the same trades in the City. To have another round about London was 'as a besieging and disconsing of the Citie thereby'. Moreover, it would tend to undermine the Leathersellers' Company, an ancient company and 'consisting of the same sort and qualities.' Moreover, Parliament

---

[5] BL Additional MS 12503. Caesar Papers.
[6] BL Additional MS 12504. Caesar Papers and Guildhall Library MS. 2915.

2   A pair of man's leather gloves with deep gauntlet cuffs and angled side vents closing with three ribbon loops. Trimmed with silk and metallic fringe, silk applique and metal thread embroidery, metallic braid and lace, 1610-25. They are believed to have been worn by James I and were subsequently owned by Ralph Thoresby, the antiquarian, and by Horace Walpole.

3   Gauntlets of the period 1600-25, one of buff coloured leather with tabs of white satin embroidered with coloured silks, gold thread and spangles in stylised rose and pansy motifs; the other of white leather with tabs of cream satin similarly embroidered in a design of whales or dolphins, trees and salamanders surmounted by strawberries, roses, tulips and carnations.

had provided[7] that the Wardens of all manual companies using leather should have power to search in London and three miles about all those cutting leather either tanned or tawed.

In any event it would be inconvenient for the City. At present there were leatherdressers and glovers living out of the City but who were free of the Leathersellers' Company and some were of the livery of that Company. A new company would draw away their apprentices who (having that alternative before them) would probably refuse to take up their freedom so as to avoid 'supporting the publick service such as are the Plantacons of Ireland, the yearly provision of corne, the provision of powder and match and the like' of which the Leathersellers bore a great proportion. Thereby that Company would be weakened and that would detract from the honour of the City.

The third objection was that the proposed incorporation was not a fit and proper one. It was too extensive as it would extend 'in compass thirty myles about'. It would be too large for good government and those concerned could be governed better and easier by the charter of the Leathersellers.

Again, it was said that it was more probable that the leatherdressers and glovers who were members of the Leathersellers' Company would provide a more effective and unbiased search of material than the petitioners who were far more likely to favour themselves and one another. In any event, the Leathersellers' Company already had a charter which gave them the right to search anywhere in England.

If those living in Southwark were included within the proposed new corporation that would be wrong. Southwark and Bermondsey were 'lymmes' of the City and the leatherdressers were planted there by a special order made for the health of the City but yet retained within the liberty and government thereof. Any inclusion of those living in Southwark would therefore infringe the City's rights.

Moreover, unless provision was made in the proposed charter of incorporation it was likely that a monopoly would be created under colour of creating good government. For whereas at present everyone could sell, dress or dispose of their wares for their best advantage that freedom might be stifled. The present system best served the public interest.

Finally, it was said that the proposed incorporation would create a precedent. Other mechanic trades would try to emulate the petitioners 'which wilbe such a rent and innovation in the City, as we may see the beginning but not hardlie discerne what wilbe the ending thereof'. This last objection was clearly an important one, which went to the heart of the matter. The petition tended to strike against the freedom of trade embodied in the custom of London in that if it was followed as a precedent by other subordinate crafts many of the established companies would be weakened by losing members and losing control of the crafts they represented. There is also a hint here that such subordinates are more suited to be governed than to govern.

All these objections inevitably drew comprehensive replies from the glovers and leatherdressers.[8] They began by answering the allegation that what was proposed was designed to create an authority which would be like a force 'besieging' or confining the City within its boundaries. It would, they said, be no more a confining of the City's

[7] Jas. I c 22.   [8] BL Additional MS 12504. Caesar Papers.

jurisdiction than was already in place by virtue of the presence of Justices of the Peace for the surrounding counties. It was a 'more souldierly than sensible' argument to put forward.

As for the suggestion that they were bent on undermining the Leathersellers' Company it was surely in their and the City's interest that their disordered neighbours should be 'drawn within government'.

They accepted that the Leathersellers' Company already included glovers and leatherdressers among its members. However, there were not more than 40 (and those only glovers) living in the City whereas the trades proposed to be incorporated were glovers, leatherdressers, vellum and parchment makers totalling three thousand. A huge number, therefore, required government. Moreover, in the case of the leatherdressers, vellum and parchment makers there were none of them living in the City because of the 'fatte and pitte' they have to use.

> Those that are now of the Leathersellers body by way of trade are one of three sorts viz eyther meere sellers of leather which is dressed and made for them by the leatherdressers and those are not above twenty masters whereof about eight (are) remarkable, or els men of a poor condicion and their workmen whom they have and use to die their leather, to withe it, pare it and sometimes for the more deceipt to stake it again or els Trunkes and Boudgettmakers such as for their materialls use only one kind of tanned shepes leather called Basills from whom may be had many testimonies of the Leathersellers' oppressions; Soe as from their aunciently united trades whereof they were aunciently compacted being leathersellers, which indeed were points and lacemakers Glovers Pursers and White tawyers they are become a body of another complexion and nature.

It was objected that there were a great number 'of the better sort' in the area of the proposed incorporation who opposed it as unnecessary and expensive. The petitioners denied that. They pointed out that it was always easy to find an objector and then it became a case of one man's word against another. Still, they could bring two in favour of incorporation for every one against and, indeed, if they could not do so the petition would not succeed. So far as the expense was concerned, if the cost of membership of the new company was heavy they would not be able to entice anyone from the freedom of London as was alleged.

To the charge that the new corporation of glovers was unnecessary because of the right of search given to the Leathersellers by charter and by statute[9] they pointed out that their concern was not merely over the right of search but about the government of their trade. There was said to be a disorderly multitude in Southwark and elsewhere who required government in all aspects of their livelihood.[10] What were needed were ordinances and an organisation to enforce them. The Leathersellers might as well be hindering the creation of a corporation of glovers in Northumberland as in the suburbs of London. They simply had not got the men able to execute a proper search and apart from a power of search they had no control whatever over those people. Their ordinances did not extend beyond the City limits. In any event, a power of search given to the new proposed corporation would supplement the search of the Leathersellers' Company.

---

[9] Jas. I c 22.   [10] See Appendix III.

If it was feared that the new company would draw off so many members of the Leathersellers' Company that that Company would be unable to pay its due contribution to the City's stock, the rejoinder was that such an event was unlikely. The new company would have no comparable privileges to offer. It could not offer the freedom of London with the prerogatives and immunities attaching.[11] On the contrary it was more likely to benefit the City by driving out poor and imperfect workmen from the City's environs who might damage the livelihood of others. And the expenses attaching to the freedom would be offset against the charges payable if they came under a new government.

The petitioners denied that they were about to create a dangerous precedent because the trades they represented could not otherwise be governed than by a new company. They could not be administered by the City because the tradesmen lived elsewhere. That was brought about partly because of the dearness of rents in the City and partly because of the noisome nature of their trade.[12] Nevertheless, they helped to maintain the City shopkeeper; for example, the glover supplied the haberdasher shopkeeper, the leatherdresser supplied the leatherseller, and the vellum and parchment maker supplied the stationer. In other trades the workers supplying the shopkeepers actually lived in the City. The new company would accept the City's governance and so the City stood to gain by the incorporation. The petitioners did not belong to the Leathersellers' Company or have the freedom of that Company. To deny the petitioners the right to incorporate would be cruel.

On the charge that the new company could quickly become a monopoly harmful to the public interest it was pointed out that their ordinances would have to be approved by the judges who would certainly not tolerate a monopoly, and furthermore they would be subject to the City's government. The petitioners could not prove the contrary case but said 'it is never safe to withstand an apparent good upon pretence of an imaginary evil'. The charter of incorporation would not require any man to be restrained or limited or directed of whom to buy or sell or for whom to dress leather. It had been said that an indication that showed monopolistic tendencies was that the petitioners wanted the right to search and seal tawed leather for the export market. That was not the case. The proposal to search tawed leather for the export market had nothing to do with the petitioners. That was a private matter concerning a patent sought by the Earl of March.[13]

It was acknowledged that the Leathersellers' Company offered to give every assistance to both the glovers and the leatherdressers for their better government and that, in fact, many leatherdressers had entered into an agreement to observe certain ordinances and pay quarterage to the Leathersellers. That could not satisfy the petitioners' grievances. If they had thought that those proposals of the Leathersellers would answer their problems they would have stayed quiet but the Leathersellers' power of search was not enough as they had shown elsewhere. The leatherdressers who had entered into an arrangement could only bind themselves. The remainder were unaffected by it.

---

[11]   By the early 14th century it was established that only members of the livery companies could become freemen of the City and enjoy the privileges which flowed from that status.
[12]   See note 17 below.
[13]   On 24 June 1620 the Attorney General announced that the Earl of March had relinquished the search of the port of London, and 'the voluntary search of any not being of this new incorporation'.

The Petitioners confessed that they were well aware that the differences within the Grocers', the Goldsmiths' and the Haberdashers' Companies had disrupted the City[14] and were still in the public mind and that similar differences existed within other companies. To this they said that if they had been resident within the City they could have given a good example to others but this ought not to be objected against them 'who haveinge no sweetnes from the Cities privileges desire only to be gathered into one fold' and they will be an example to others when it is seen what 'poore people as the Glovers and Leatherdressers hold themselves blessed by enioying hereby but the shadow of their felicity'.

Then it was argued that if a new corporation was created it would simply attract more strangers to it. The concern of the authorities was to stop the flow of people coming in from the country to the suburbs 'least too much of the humours of the body should be attracted to the head'. This would not follow the new incorporation unless it was made unduly attractive as by giving it the right to hold fairs or markets or by giving it special immunities. Otherwise, the cost of joining the company would deter those who saw no corresponding benefits to induce them to leave their present homes. A chief purpose of the incorporation was to provide enforceable rules governing the acceptance and training of apprentices, the employment of journeymen and the standards required of a master. Now there were no enforceable rules and no recognised standards.

Likewise, it was accepted that the Leathersellers' Company was prepared to admit a number of the 'fittest' glovers and leatherdressers to further their desired government if that would suffice and avoid a new incorporation. In fact, those acceptable to the Leathersellers were precisely those who needed no 'government' and to give through them a power to govern the rest was so strange as to be able to give others that ability which they themselves have not'. If the Leathersellers had the power to govern they need not call such people in aid.

Southwark, where most glovers and leatherdressers lived was, indeed, a 'limb of London'. It was within the City's jurisdiction but for matters of public order rather than for matters of trade. 'Foreigners' could trade there as easily as elsewhere. The petitioners did not intend to detract from the City's authority. The new company would exclude all existing freemen within its circuit unless they wished to join it. The petitioners desired only to take upon themselves the government and order of the rest in point of trade where they were not then governed. To deprive the petitioners both of the freedom of the City on the one hand and the right of self government on the other was to leave them in debatable land where those concerned could ignore all power and authority and, indeed, the worst sort of person could take advantage of the situation to contribute to disorder.

This counterblast by the glovers and leatherdressers was not complete. Some of their observations were supplemented by additional arguments.[15] It had been suggested that at the heart of the problem lay the continuing difficulty of providing an effective search and seal to root out defective leather and shoddy wares. 'Foreigners' ought to be

---

[14] i.e. the disputes between the Apothecaries and the Grocers and between the Gold and Silver Wyre Drawers and the Goldsmiths and between the Feltmakers and the Haberdashers.
[15] BL Additional MS 12504. Caesar Papers.

encouraged to participate in a voluntary search and seal. If they could be persuaded to do that much of the basis of complaint would disappear. The petitioners would have none of this. A voluntary search and seal would be a waste of time, a 'plaine folly'. Men were not going to pay for something without real benefits ensuing. Nevertheless, if once a voluntary search was established it would soon be made compulsory at the instance of those who submitted to a voluntary search for their private ends. A compulsory search would, of course, have to be capable of being enforced and, in the circumstances, that could only be done by the proposed incorporation. 'For the voluntaries it is but *timor nocturnis* or *timidia nequitia*[16] judging us by their standards. It is better to meet that complaint when and if it arises than to hinder a lawful exercise by imaginary future mischief.'

They explained that the leatherdressers (mainly white tawyers) had been excluded from the City by public order on the grounds of creating a danger to the health of their fellow citizens since the time of King Edward IV.[17] These craftsmen

> with whom the Leathersellers usage is somewhat considerable in their offers to us that having promised them they should ever be esteemed of their bodie; yet having once translated them by this public order from the local circuit of their jurisdiction they have in process of time wormed them out of their freedom, allowing none of the breed and posterity of their workmen to be free, to whom they made so large a promise there not being at this day a leatherdresser free of the Leathersellers' Company. Although to give some colourable answer to this they would blind your Lordshipp with a few Fellmongers who neither doe nor know how to dresse skins into leather; but if they durst would cast the pelt upon the dunghill having before suckt out their profitt by pulling off sorting and selling the wooll.

The petitioners had asked that the area to be covered by their corporation should be for a radius of seven miles around the City. It was said that that was too extensive but the petitioners replied that in fact most of the craftsmen were concentrated in a few areas. If the area was too large for the new corporation armed with proper ordinances it was clear that it was beyond the governing powers of the Leathersellers' Company. They had to rely on an ineffective power of search rendered more ineffective because 'none of that Company know the secret imperfections of leatherdressing much less of any made wares'.

To a further objection to incorporation filed on behalf of the Leathersellers (stressing that their right to search was all over England and would be unbiased) the petitioners responded that nothing they were doing could alter or abrogate the rights of the Leathersellers. They could use their power to search the goods of the petitioners whether corporated or unincorporated. 'We shall be heartily glad if they will survey our enormities if they will take the pains and have the power.'

Finally, the glovers pointed out that other trades had a body of workmen resident within the City. However, and here the Leathersellers who for their private ends opposed the petition should be ashamed, whereas in other trades 'the shopkeepers growing rich make the workmen their underlings yet suffer them to prosper to become like themselves

---

[16] Fear of the night or of evil.
[17] It is said that the trade of whittawyer or leatherdresser was more noisome even than that of the tanner in that the latter took the skins of slaughtered cattle while the former often used the skins of animals which had died naturally. See Roy Thomson, 'Leather manufacture in the post-medieval period with special reference to Northamptonshire' in *Post-medieval Archaeology*, 15 (1981), 161-75.

and in the meantime to receive the favour of the Company', that was not the system which prevailed between Leathersellers and Glovers. While in other trades

> some shopkeepers though they sell the workmen their material yet they take it back when manufactured at reasonable rates as, e.g. Goldsmiths, Skinners and Silkmen, yet the Leathersellers, though they profess to be of the same trade as us, if they once put their griping hands between grower and merchant they never part with any of the commodities they buy without selling them at pitched rates without any regard or care whether ever the workman be able to make his money thereof or noe ... so as whether we be respected as we are inhabiting without the freedom and none of our trades exercised within the same ... or as the Leathersellers having iniuriously driven us from our seats within the City and liberties are like changelings in our cradle alienated from the nature or knowledge of our trades and so incapable of government as through ignorance.

There could be no question of creating a precedent since the Glovers were in a completely different position from any of the other mechanic trades either within the City or its suburbs. 'Therefore, as macerated obiects of the Leathersellers' envie who, not contented to possess our *patrias sedes*,[18] yet grudge we should have any place of being elsewhere. We hope rather to deserve pity than persecution which we most humbly beseech your Lordshipps would with tenderness consider.'

If the facts set out in these replies (and particularly those set out in the last paragraph) are true it tends to confirm Unwin's point that 'It made the nominal share of the handicraft members in the Company's freedom less and less of a reality, while at the same time it lent increasing force to their demand for a separate incorporation.'[19]

The answers and objections followed each other in rapid succession. It may be that the Leathersellers' Company followed up their original objections to the proposed incorporation with a revised list. At any rate, no less than three different sets of answers to these objections are lodged in the British Library. Possibly one or more were merely drafts but there is a wide variation of wording and emphasis.

However, the petitioners failed to achieve their object and it was to be 15 years before they tried again. It is clear that there was a great deal of discontent in the air and an urgent need that perceived abuses should be reformed. An example of the circumstances which provoked protest was provided in 1621. The leatherdressers of Southwark, with whom the glovers were aligned, petitioned the Solicitor General to take action to safeguard their livelihood. Strangers, Dutchmen, who had never served a proper apprenticeship, were engaged in the trade. To add insult to injury these Dutchmen bluntly said they would employ whom they pleased how they pleased. It was a great grievance that 'strangers should have greater privileges that the native English may claim' and, not unnaturally, the result was that the leatherdressers' own apprentices were reluctant to complete their term and were tempted to go to these strangers.

The following year they addressed another petition to the Surrey Justices.[20] This time they named Peeter de Vons, a Dutchman, who, they said, never completed his own apprenticeship yet employed unqualified journeymen in defiance of all the attempts of

---

[18]   Literally, the seats of our fathers; our inheritance.   [19]   Unwin, *Industrial Organisation*, p.128.
[20]   Public Record Office (Hereafter PRO) State Papers Domestic (SPD) 14/127 f.30.

the petitioners to persuade him to do otherwise. Indeed, he employed aliens and strangers and had 'put away' ancient workmen that served their time and paid their dues. That was not their only complaint. They alleged that Henry de Vons (Peeter's brother) and Henrick, his servant, had fathered bastards which they would not maintain, and that Peeter traded not only as a leatherdresser but as a distiller of *aquavite*,[21] and as a fuller, though it is not entirely clear which was the gravest offence. Peeter, in his answer, had pointed out that his dressing of 'oyle' leather[22] was a new trade which the Dutch had introduced into England but the leatherdressers while conceding that the Dutch brought in the dressing of buff hides[23] into 'oyle' leather said that buckskins, stagg skins,[24] goatskins, sheepskins and lambskins were always dressed in England and belonged to the trade of glovers and leatherdressers. How the matter ended is not disclosed. No doubt an accommodation of sorts was reached between the parties.

---

[21] The water of life; any form of ardent spirits as, for example, brandy.
[22] The whittawyer or leatherdresser took the skins of animals other than cattle and processed them using alum and oil. By the 16th century he also used vegetable materials. For the production of chamois and buff leathers fish oil would be used in their preparation. See Roy Thomson, 'Leather manufacture in the post-medieval period ...', *supra*.
[23] A stout kind of leather made of ox hide dressed with oil.
[24] A male animal, for example, a male of a deer, a bull, boar or ram.

V

The Glovers Gain Their Charter

IT IS INSTRUCTIVE to consider the claims and arguments put forward by the glovers and leatherdressers from the viewpoint of the Leathersellers' Company and the City authorities. The minute books of the Leathersellers' Company survive covering the period in question. An entry dated 8 July 1611[1] shows that the trade of glovers was 'much decaied' and few of that art then remained (in the Company) so that the search could not be duly executed and there were 'manifold abuses in the cutting and making of gloves and purses'. On the other hand many foreigners residing in the suburbs exercised the trade. It was resolved that an application should be made to the Court of Aldermen that 20 'forraines' who were able and skilful should be admitted free of the Company to rectify the position. That application was, as mentioned earlier, granted the following year and it illustrates the fact that, so far as they could, the Company supported the demands of the glovers and leatherdressers within its ranks excepting always the demand for independence which it could not concede.

On 18 June 1613[2] it was agreed that 'forraigne working glovers' might bind their apprentices to freemen of the Company and then set them over to their working masters again so that in due course on completion of their term of apprenticeship they might be made free of the Leathersellers' Company. This was a further attempt to increase the number of freemen glovers of the Company.

The Court of Assistants was ready to be helpful in other ways as well. For example, in 1621 it was agreed that the free glovers who were free of any other City company might meet in the yeomanry parlour so long as 'one of our manualls be present with them'.

More importantly, on 12 January 1625[3] the Court set up a committee to join in 'debate and conference' with the foreign glovers for a reconciliation and government under the Company of Leathersellers by mutual consent. In fact the differences were so great that no such reconciliation was possible.

The Repertories of the Court of Aldermen are a further source of information about the progress of the Glovers' petition for a charter of incorporation. Perhaps they reveal also the attitude of the City which, initially at any rate, tended to support the Leathersellers and the preservation of the status quo.

As early as 1622,[4] Thomas Tyler and Robert Freeman of the Leathersellers' Company petitioned the Court of Aldermen for payment of the substantial sum of £380 which they had disbursed 'in defence of a project to erect a Company and corporation of

---

[1] Minute book of the Leathersellers' Company 1608-22.
[2] ibid.
[3] Minute book of the Leathersellers' Company 1623-32.
[4] CLRO REP 36.

leatherdressers, glovers and others using and dealing in leather'. The Court referred the matter to a committee who should call before them the Master and Wardens of the Leathersellers' Company and treat with them for payment of the money. Evidently it was felt that the Leathersellers' defence was also a defence of the City's privileges and merited a joint approach. It was, of course, perceived by both parties as a dangerous precedent which other workers might seek to emulate and which, if unchecked, would strike ultimately against all the established companies and the freedom they enjoyed of embracing members using a multiplicity of trades.

Mr. Freeman had met with some difficulty within the ranks of his own Company where the minutes show that various fellmongers, leatherdressers, trunkmakers[5] and glovers appeared and refused to contribute towards his 'great charge'.

Later, at the request of the Leathersellers' Company, the Court of Aldermen was represented at hearings before the Privy Council and the Attorney General.

The desire of the glovers and leatherdressers to have their own company and to rule themselves could not be satisfied by consultation and discussion, however well meant. In the 1630s their petition for a separate incorporation was renewed. The Leathersellers were sufficiently alarmed to appoint a committee in October 1634 to confer with their members who were trading leathersellers or glovers to discover if the government of the Society might be threatened thereby and, if so, 'speedy course bee taken to stopp the same'.[6]

In July 1635[7] it was reported that the Glovers' petition had been lodged and the King had referred it to the Attorney General for his opinion. The Attorney had set down a date and time for the parties to appear before him. The Court of the Leathersellers decided that the Master, Wardens and some half dozen senior members of the Company supported by counsel should be present bringing with them the Company's charters and ordinances.

By August it was clear that the defence of their rights might prove costly. It was reported that most trading leathersellers were free of other companies such as the Haberdashers or the Vintners. It was resolved[8] that those companies should be asked whether they would support their members who were trading leathersellers in paying the costs of opposing the glovers. If any company should refuse to assist such a member and if such member himself refused to pay his share of the costs an application would then be made to the Court of Aldermen that any such trading leatherseller desiring the Company's assistance should be translated from his own company to the Leathersellers' Company. In the meantime further steps in the defence of the Glovers' petition should be taken and they would present to the Attorney General 'twenty peeces as a gratuity from our Socyety for his paines taking in and about the same'. The trading leathersellers were invited to attend at Leathersellers' Hall where it was indicated to them that they ought to contribute to the costs incurred by the Leathersellers' Company or else that Company would endeavour to have them translated to it.

In due course three liverymen of the Haberdashers' Company, two of the Goldsmiths', one of the Skinners' and one of the Clothworkers' appeared. They gave the

---

5   By this date pouchmakers and budgetmakers were known as trunkmakers.
6   Minute book of the Leathersellers' Company 1632-50.
7   ibid.   8   ibid.

Company 'greate thanks for theire care in prosecuting (the defence)'. They acknowledged that such action benefited the whole trade and all agreed to contribute their share of the expenses and, if necessary, they would willingly be translated from their own companies.

Even at this stage of events it is clear that not all working glovers had aligned themselves with the petitioners. In January 1636[9] the minute books of the Leathersellers record that a deputation of glovers first asked if they might undertake a search of gloves and other wares made of leather and have the use of the yeomanry parlour with a member or members of the livery present but then, for some unexplained reason, withdrew their request. Nevertheless, the Company, being desirous to carry out its obligations in regard to the search and sealing of leather appointed one Humphrey Aston, 'an experienced glover', to undertake the search and seal on behalf of the Company for one year. For his better encouragement the Company agreed to pay Aston £10. A member of the Leathersellers' livery was appointed to assist him and they were to share equally the proceeds from all forfeitures.

Again, in May of that year[10] the Wardens and senior members of the livery were required to hold monthly meetings with the trading glovers 'as well free as forraigne' to consider the grievances and abuses committed in the trade and so that some speedy course might be taken to punish the same.

Around this time the action taken by the petitioning glovers seems to have fallen into abeyance and the only reference to such ongoing proceedings is a motion[11] that a gratuity should be paid to Sir John Banks, the Attorney General, 'concerning a favour done on behalf of the Society'. The amount is not mentioned.

In the end the Glovers succeeded through Court influence and because the Crown was sympathetic to their cause. According to Unwin, monopolies not only provided the King with money but enabled him to reward his servants and friends while at the same time encouraging native industries, protecting the small manufacturer from the domination of the capitalist and providing sound goods at reasonable rates.[12] Unwin also asserts that the idea of protecting the poorer industrial classes was a real motive of Stuart policy.[13]

On this occasion the Glovers were able to enlist the aid of a courtier, Lady Killigrew, who was hoping for a patent similar to that granted to Mr. Darcy. In June 1636 she petitioned the King in support of the Glovers.[14] Her petition showed that the glovers about London, 'being a great company of poore men', had previously presented their own petition complaining of the great decay of their trade because of frauds in dressing tawed leather and the great oppression caused by a few Leathersellers in engrossing all sorts of leather and then selling it at extraordinary rates to the glovers who had no means of telling whether the skins they were getting were good or bad because of the way they were packed for sale. They had therefore asked the King to incorporate them as a separate Company and to grant them the right to search and seal all tawed leather 'with allowance of moderate fees for the same'.

The King had referred the Glovers' petition to the Attorney General who heard both the Glovers and the Leathersellers with their counsel and eventually 'it was agreed

---

[9] ibid. [10] ibid. [11] ibid.
[12] Unwin, *Gilds and Companies*, p.293. [13] Unwin, *Industrial Organisation*, p.143. [14] PRO SPD 16/323 f.15.

by all and consented unto by the Leathersellers' that the Glovers should be incorporated and that there should be a search and seal for all leather for their use. 'And yet the said Leathersellers for the meynteynance of theire unlawfull gaines did use all possible meanes to hinder the certificate of your Majesty's Attorney Generall by suborning diveres complaintes in the agreement to the said search and seale.' Eventually the King commanded the Attorney General to make his report and he had done so approving a corporation for the Glovers for a radius of three miles about London with a right of search and seal of all leather useful for their manufacture and with an allowance to charge moderate fees in connection therewith.

However, alleged Lady Killigrew, the Leathersellers still persisted in their opposition saying that they themselves had a power to view and search leather within three miles of London and they now began to exercise that right 'which they have not formerly used within the memory of man' and, in addition, they said they had new information to lay before the King in support of their case. On the contrary she pointed out that because the abuse and fraud in dressing leather for the Glovers' use was so general and universal all over the kingdom and because the Leathersellers were 'notorious offenders and oppressors' she intended to proceed against them in the Court of Star Chamber.

She therefore besought the King to order the Attorney General to prepare a grant of incorporation for the Glovers to extend four miles about London as in the case of the corporation granted to the Feltmakers' Company and to grant the search and seal to such as she should nominate to her use, such search not to be confined to a three-mile radius of London but to be general and for all leather useful for the manufacture of gloves, a similar larger grant having been made by Queen Elizabeth to one of her servants.[15] She also asked for an allowance of a search fee which she said was not more than half that allowed by Queen Elizabeth.

As a result of Lady Killigrew's petition, questions relating to the kinds of leather to be viewed and sealed, the fees to be charged and the radius and extent of the proposed corporation were referred to a committee of the Privy Council. The Attorney General might then draw up the incorporation.

At this stage of events there was an outbreak of the plague in London[16] and all proceedings to incorporate the Glovers came to a halt. They were not renewed until March 1638.

Again the Glovers were obliged to reiterate the substance of their claim for incorporation.[17] They reminded the Privy Council that they had petitioned to be incorporated for seven miles about London but that it was proposed to restrict them to a circuit of three miles. That would not solve their problem because many who were 'refractory' at the trade would thereby be excluded 'and yet neere London'. As a result the abuses complained of would largely remain unreformed. Besides, the Leathersellers' corporation was not restricted to three miles about London.

The Leathersellers, still contesting the issue, urged that bazelles[18] ought not to be sealed but the Glovers asked the Council to distinguish between tanned and tawed material.

---

[15] i.e. Mr. Darcy.   [16] In June 1636.   [17] PRO SPD 16/377 f.63.
[18] Rough tanned sheepskins used for shoe linings. See Roy Thomson, 'Leather manufacture in the post-medieval period ...', *supra*.

It was very necessary to search and seal tawed bazelles. Tanned bazelles were not made to endure stress. They were made to line the skirts of saddles, the insides of girdles and to paste on trunks,[19] or to provide stiffening for other materials. On the other hand, tawed leather was to be worn single and had to endure all weathers. If it was badly dressed it tore and rotted. Tawed leather had long been subject to a strict search and it was used for gloves, purses, points, pockets and bags, etc.

There were 500 tawed skins to every tanned bazelle, such skins being the sole materials for the glovers' use.

The Leathersellers feared that if the Glovers were given the right to search and seal leather it would disclose the full extent of their malpractices in engrossing leather. In fact the Leathersellers willingly paid Sir Thomas Glover a fee of 1s. 4d. for sealing every 100 skins they exported. Aliens were therefore better protected than native craftsmen who had to buy leather which might have been badly dressed. The Leathersellers, said the Glovers, contradict themselves. At one point they say it costs them £10 a year to carry out their search of leather and at another they say they perform the search for nothing. In October 1634 they did make a search with the aid of some glovers. Out of 80 dozen gloves inspected 34 dozen were condemned in the Sheriff's Court as defective wares. The King should have a half of all defective wares but the Glovers now wonder if on this or any other occasion he received any benefit.

The Leathersellers had said that they had a power of search under a statute passed in the first year of King James I's reign but that statute did not mention either leathersellers or glovers or glovers' work such as gloves, purses, points, pockets or bags but rather the trades using tanners' leather. It was plainly expressed to refer to whatsoever wares were made of tanned leather and glovers did not use tanned leather. The Glovers then went on to explain to their Lordships of the Privy Council what was meant by the term leatherseller. They describe 'the distinction and character of the Company called Leathersellers and of the hucksters or sellers of leather'.

Firstly, they say that Company was incorporated a brotherhood in the sixth and twenty-second years of Richard II's reign being then 'micanicks, Glovers, Pursers and Longe Cutters (that is Point makers) and for unityes sake called Leathersellers, that is such as made, drest and sold wares of tawed leather'. King Henry VII had confirmed their status with power to search all over England for tawed leather, gloves, points or purses, etc. Because of the custom of London the Company had long ago changed in character to those unconnected to the trade of leather. Generally, the Master and Wardens were men practising other trades as, for example, braziers, hosiers or falconers so that for a long time the search of tawed leather had been omitted or badly performed 'to the greate abuse of the commonwealth'.

Secondly, they say that those they describe as hucksters or sellers of leather had their beginnings about 50 years ago. Before that there were none in London who merely bought leather and sold it again in the same state without working on it and there are none such in any other part of the kingdom. There were three or four of these hucksters

---

[19] i.e. pouches.

at the most, namely, Waplayd, by trade a falconer's bag maker, Barlow, a clothworker, and Ward, who was free of the Leathersellers. Ward took as his apprentice Mr. Freeman who they regard as the great opposer of their petition for incorporation. From these people had emerged all the petty sellers of leather who by Mr. Freeman's endeavours borrowed colour from the Leathersellers' Company to oppose the Glovers. Such people, although they supported Mr. Freeman, were men of other trades and companies as, for example, Mr. Tyler and Mr. Alcock, by trade stationers and by company Haberdashers, and Mr. Shellesbury, by trade a scrivener but free of another company. These were men who had been buying up all foreign and native commodities for nearly 20 years. The whole trade of glovers was aware of and could confirm the engrossing of foreign goods. Confirmation that they engrossed native leather was evidenced by a certificate from Salisbury. The Leathersellers themselves confirmed that the best leather was exported by them. There were no goats' or kids' leather to be found anywhere but in the hands of Mr. Freeman, Mr. Tyler and Mr. Alcock. They worked together as one man and in 1625 they passed through the Port of London nearly 50,000 sheep and lamb skins which would have kept 200 people in work for a year and brought six times more benefit in customs duties in the manufacture of gloves than was produced simply from the material of leather itself.

The next point made by the Glovers concerned leather brought to London from the provinces. The Leathersellers argued that leather which arrived from Bristol or Chester was transported in packs by carriers which the carriers would have to unload (no doubt at great trouble) for a thorough search to be carried out but, just as the hatmakers had a right of search for materials brought in, so should the Glovers be enabled to inspect their leather as otherwise there would be no way of getting rid of the abuses. Leather from Bristol or Chester was brought 'in the crust' as it was termed. That is to say it arrived dried and hard from exposure to the weather and that made it difficult to discover frauds. As an example, William Trusse, a glover, paid £34 for a parcel of leather but found £10 worth valueless.

Finally, they said that while they understood that the Attorney General was a very busy man they hoped their Lordships would urge that other counsel should join him in settling the grant of incorporation, 'it being an action of that greate consequence which concernes thousandes of his Majestes subjectes and both the improvement of trade and of his Majestes Customes'.

There is among the State Papers another version of the statement made at this time by the Glovers in support of their petition. In large measure the two statements overlap but there are occasional differences which make it unclear which was regarded as the final case to put before the Privy Council. The alternative statement[20] does include a separate schedule of reasons for the proposed incorporation.

Firstly, it should be established in Westminster because nearly all the Glovers live outside the City liberties. They keep no shops there but sell their goods to the haberdashers.

Secondly, there are great abuses in the trade. Some employers take as many as seven or eight apprentices as well as boys and runaways from all parts of the kingdom and

---

[20] PRO SPD 11/386 f.164.

'women dayly taught for money the makinge of gloves to the increase of a burthensome and disordered multitude … greately hynderinge the sale of such ware in forraigne partes to the damage of his Majesties Customes and beggarye of the trade'.

Thirdly, many trades of less consequence have been incorporated including some that seem to be under the control of others, such as the Hatmakers which are under the Haberdashers' Company with power to search hats and caps and the material required to make them. King James gave the foreign hatmakers about London a corporation with a like power of search because, being artists, they were best able to judge frauds and certify abuses of the trade.

And fourthly, incorporation would benefit the Crown because if leather was duly sealed good materials might be had without which good wares could not be made.

There follows a statement setting out reasons why the sealing of leather is regarded as so essential.

First of all it was necessary as a safeguard of quality. Whereas the shoemaker knew where to have his remedy if his leather proved to be faulty, the glover did not. The glover did not buy directly from the dresser but from an intermediary. He could not buy it anywhere else and he had to take it as it came often at excessive rates and without any seal as to its quality.

The allegation of the poor quality of packs arriving 'in crust',[21] with no means of distinguishing good from bad is repeated. It was said that 'the hucksters of leather' slipped into a parcel of a dozen kidskins or goatskins worth between 10s. and 14s. a dozen a murrain[22] skin not worth a penny. If all skins had to be sealed this practice would not survive. That it was prevalent is shown by the number of gloves condemned in the Sheriff's Court.

Even aliens had benefits denied to the native English, some of whom were consequently forced to go over to Holland and other parts because they could not make a living here. At present these 'hucksters' by their intervention were destroying the trade of the leatherdressers by making them their servants and employees and damaging the trade of the glovers. Their actions were contrary to statute.[23] They ought either to pay others to examine and seal the skins or leave them to the petitioners to arrange and they would pay such sums as were due to his Majesty immediately. The petitioners proposed a charge for sealing at the rate of 1s. for every 100 skins which was less than Sir Thomas Glover's fee and much less than the fee granted to Mr. Darcy by Queen Elizabeth which amounted to 2s. 6d. for a dozen skins. Such skins were sold on average for £4 for every 100 skins and therefore the fee worked out at about 3d. in the pound for sealing. 'The paines to search a dozen of this is as much as in a dicker[24] of tanners leather because the fraudes are generallye greater and the skynns might be turned over severallye.'

The Glovers then summed up the position claiming that they number about 5,000 persons about London (although elsewhere they claim to number 8,000 persons and in a third instance 'above four hundred housekeepers and above three thousand dependinge

---

[21] Dried from exposure to the weather.   [22] From an animal which had died of disease.
[23] 5 Eliz. c 22.
[24] Half a score. The word has been used from ancient times in the reckoning of hides and skins.

on them of servantes workeinge on gloves'). They recalled how the Attorney General held several hearings and that it was eventually thought fit that the Glovers should have a search and seal for all leather useful for their trade but limited to within three miles of London with moderate fees. However, no fees were fixed because that matter was not referred to the Attorney General.

Now the Glovers wished all to be concluded. They hoped that their incorporation could be formally granted in accordance with the Attorney General's recommendation but that the search and seal might be all over England and for all kinds of tawed leather (tanned leather being already sealed by Act of Parliament), such search and seal being 'first setled' in London and seven miles round about. They asked that their fees be those set out in their petition. They referred to the bill exhibited by Lady Killigrew against the Leathersellers in the Star Chamber prosecuted at the petitioners' charge. They concluded by desiring the King to command the Attorney General to take care of the bill 'and to prosecute it for your Majestie's service the offenders being very rich men and able to yeld your Majestie greate fines answerable to their offences'.

At last the Glovers were successful. At a meeting of the Privy Council on 29 April 1638[25] they received formal approval of their petition to become a corporate body of men. Even now, however, there was a problem. The charter of incorporation which is dated 10 September was drawn in such a way that they felt they could not make use of it. There was, they said,[26] 'no place named where our corporation shalbe laide', only that they be incorporated for three miles about London. All over the country there were many towns with companies of Glovers 'incorporate' in them but even now there was no such company in London where the trade abuses were most manifest. Later that year the Glovers therefore went back to the Privy Council to try to get this alleged defect put right. They said, 'we beseech your lordships to take pitty on this soe much admired manufacture abroad in the English nation and so much neglected and decayed at home that we may see some end of it'.

No doubt their lordships echoed that pious hope. In fact, no further amendment seems to have been made to the charter which is dated 10 September 14 Chas I.[27] The Glovers failed in several of their requests, most notably in the desire for their authority to extend in a seven-mile radius of London, and to obtain authority to charge search fees of any kind and to have the search extended to all tawed leather. The Glovers could hardly complain that the charter did not stipulate that they should be incorporated within the City since the whole tenor of their claim was based on the fact that scarcely any of them lived or worked in the City; they were living and working in the suburbs round about.

---

[25]   PRO Privy Council papers. 2/49 f.149.
[26]   PRO SPD 16/407 f.95.   [27]   i.e. 1638. Guildhall Library MS 4594.

VI

The Charter is Enrolled by the City

IT SOON BECAME APPARENT that mere incorporation was not enough to satisfy the needs of the new Company. The most obvious difficulty was that of enforcing control over the members and arranging for apprentices to be made free of the City. It was necessary to have the Company of Glovers admitted as one of the recognised City companies, so that the authority of the Master and Wardens could be backed up by the Court of Aldermen to whom the officers of the Company could look for recognition of their ordinances. Moreover, all apprentices could then be brought before the Chamberlain to be made free of the City before being admitted to the Company. [1]

In the spring of 1641 the Glovers launched a further petition.[2] This time it was addressed to the Court of Aldermen. They sought, in the words of the Repertories, to be 'reduced to a Brotherhood'.[3] As was its practice, the Court of Aldermen appointed a committee to consider the petition and report. The committee heard the representatives not only of the Glovers but also those of the Leathersellers who maintained their opposition to this further move to establish the Company of Glovers within the City's ranks.

In August the minutes of the Leathersellers' Company[4] reveal that their Court had been notified of the petition in which the Glovers had stressed the need to search for deceitful gloves and leather. The Leathersellers had reminded the Court of Aldermen that they already had full rights of searching and sealing and proceedings had been adjourned to enable both parties to be heard by counsel. The court of the Leathersellers' Company seems to have been alarmed, fearing that the Glovers might have further designs which might prove harmful. It was resolved that, 'taking into consideration and knowing that the working Glovers have ever endeavoured to disquyett and trouble our Society with uniust vexacons, they being most of them poore and very clamourous', the Master and Wardens, assisted by no less than 16 of the livery (including the celebrated Mr. Freeman and the gentleman who became ever more celebrated as Praise-God Barebones)[5] 'and the working Glovers free of our Society', be ordered to advise and consider how the business

---

[1] The Chamberlain has for centuries exercised jurisdiction in respect of apprentices bound by London Indenture and the Chamberlain's court has entertained complaints by either master or apprentice. Unruly apprentices could be committed to Bridewell for periods up to three months. The admission of freemen was always one of the duties of the Chamberlain. Jones, *The Corporation of London*, pp.90-1.

[2] CLRO REP 55.

[3] This involved the enrolment of the Company's charter by the Court of Aldermen. An Act of Parliament of 1437 (15 Henry VI c 6), confirmed by charter to the City in 1505, required letters patent of guilds, fraternities and incorporated companies to be registered before the Justices of the Peace for the counties and the chief governors of cities and towns. 'The result is that today the terms of charters of incorporation are approved by the Court of Aldermen before submission to the Privy Council to ensure that they do not infringe City customs.' Jones, *The Corporation of London*, pp.46-7.

[4] Minute book of the Leathersellers' Company 1632-50.

[5] He was a Common Councillor for the Ward of Farringdon Without in 1650-1 and 1658-60. Jones, *The Corporation of London*, p.14.

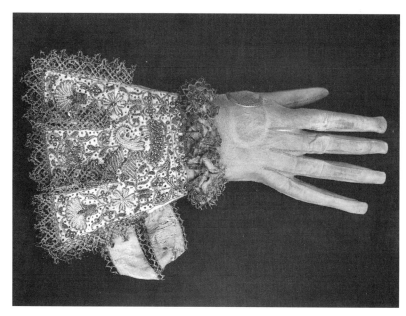

4   Buff leather glove with tabs of cream satin embroidered with silk cord, gold thread, seed pearls and spangles in a design of carnations, roses and, possibly, cornflowers surmounting the pelican in her piety, 1610-30.

5   Gloves of leather and doeskin of the period 1630-80 variously decorated with coloured silk ribbons and trimmed with silver gilt thread and braid, lace and spangles, embroidered on green silk thread and trimmed or ornamented with loops or rosettes of silk.

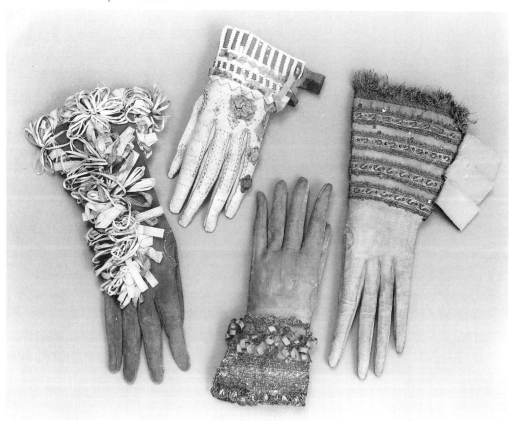

could be prosecuted to effect. At the same time the Court of Aldermen was investigating the background to the Glovers' petition. After reviewing the history of the Company the committee reported,[6] 'wee find that the Glovers are exceedingly increased in number and abilityes and that their trade is now more of consequence than formerly … and that their commodity is much transported and of much esteeme in forreine parts'. They recognised the necessity of enforcing an effective search and that the Glovers' only desire was that their charter should be enrolled so that they might be termed as anciently they were, 'Cittizens and Glovers of London'. Thereby the government of the Company might be more regular and effective and abuses brought under control 'by having the assistance of this Court'.

The committee were unconvinced by the Leathersellers' argument that it was unnecessary to enrol the Charter because their own powers were adequate. The committee took the view that the Glovers were better qualified to judge the materials and workmanship of their own goods than the Leathersellers were; that since the Leathersellers still acted as middlemen in the sale of leather they might not be over rigorous in their search and that, in any event, nothing was being taken from the Leathersellers. At the most the search was being duplicated. After all, a double search was not something new. It applied to other goods and to other trades. The committee went on to find as a fact that numbers of Glovers were free of some of the greatest of the City Companies, that they did not seek to be severed from such Companies without the free consent of such Company and that they did not seek to force members of other companies to bind their apprentices to those free of the Glovers' Company. That impressed the committee. They recognised that there was no attempt to weaken or to wrong any other Company. The committee was prepared to recommend acceptance of the petition pointing out that it was more in the nature of a restoration than the creation of a new company. In addition, it was not prejudicial to the City financially but, rather, beneficial since the Glovers were content to pay scot and lot[7] as 'shalbe agreeable to their abilities'. They recommended that the Charter should be enrolled.

The Court of Aldermen took note of this and appointed a date when the Master and Wardens of the Leathersellers' Company might be heard. There were numerous adjournments after this because of the failure of the Leathersellers to attend a hearing and it was not until 1644 that matters were brought to finality.

In May the Leathersellers' Court again considered the matter.[8] A strong deputation was named to oppose the enrolment of the Glovers' charter 'which may in tyme prove prejuidicial to our Society'.

In October yet another committee was appointed by the Court of Aldermen to consider every particular of the Glovers' charter and the 'conveniency and inconveniency' of enrolling it.[9] They reported back within the same month that there was nothing in the

---

[6] CLRO REP 55.
[7] Each householder was required to repair and sweep his frontage to the kennel in the centre of the road, to hang out a light during the dark evenings, to provide a bucket of water at his door during the dry season and to act in turn with the other householders as scavenger, beadle and constable. The performance of such duties was called 'bearing lot'. The payment of rates in lieu of personal service whereby permanent employees could be engaged was termed 'paying scot'. Jones, *The Corporation of London*, p.125.
[8] Minute book of the Leathersellers' Company 1632-50.   [9] CLRO REP 57.

charter which would entitle any Glover who was not free of the City to claim the freedom thereby or that sought to separate either then or in the future from the Company of Leathersellers or from any other Company any Glovers free of such Company, nor to give them any pretence to withdraw their allegiance. Particularly, there was no suggestion of any claim to the land, goods or chattels of the Leathersellers or any other Company. On the contrary, the benefit sought by the enrolment was the better government of the Glovers' Company.

That seems to have been sufficient. It was ordered[10] that the Charter be enrolled.

It is interesting to observe that the Court of Aldermen arranged through its good offices a reconciliation between the two Companies. On 27 January 1647[11] a motion by Mr. Serjeant Greene, the Recorder, 'for a reconciliation and agreement of the cause of difference' between the Leathersellers and the Glovers was heard. It was ordered that a petition recently received from the Glovers' Company should be subscribed by the Master, Wardens and Assistants of that Company and that that document along with another under the common seal of the Glovers' Company, purporting to release to the Leathersellers any claim which they or their members might enjoy against the property of that Company, be entered in the Repertory.

The Glovers were ordered to bring into the Chamber of London the names of all glovers who were free of the Company and the names of their bound apprentices, and it was ordered that no glover free of the Leathersellers' Company (except such as willingly will of themselves) might be compelled to make oath to the Glovers' Company or pay their quarterage. Thereupon the Glovers should be able to enrol their apprentices in the Chamber of London and afterwards make them free of the City.

The petition of the Glovers' Company referred to began by thanking the Court of Aldermen for the enrolment of its Charter and other favours tending to the better government of their manufacture, but asked that they might be permitted to enrol their apprentices at the Guildhall and also to translate to their Company any members voluntarily bestowed upon them by any other company. At the same time they offered to release all claims and demands they might possibly have against any property of the Leathersellers' Company in such form as the Court of Aldermen or that Company might reasonably require.

The form of release is also set out in the Repertory.[12] It recites that the Company has been a fellowship and brotherhood for 'tyme whereof there is no memorie of man to the contrary', the granting of their Charter in the 14th year of Charles I, and the form of the petition. It goes on to say, 'to cleere all doubts and obiections', that the Company

> remised, released and quit claimed to the Leathersellers' Company all right, title, pretence of title, interest, claim or demand whatsoever to the great Common Hall or any of the manors, messuages, lands, annuities, tenements and hereditaments, goods, chattels and other real and personal estate whatsoever of that Company and the Company of Glovers be thereafter debarred from all such claims and demands ... And as concerning the desire of the Leathersellers' Company to be eased of part of their proportion of corn allotted upon them and to be layed upon the Glovers this Court will hereafter take the same into consideration.

---

[10] ibid.   [11] CLRO REP 59.   [12] ibid.

6 Tradesmen preachers in the City of London. From a Broadside 1647.

That release marked the final termination of the long drawn out dispute between the Leathersellers and the Glovers. Henceforth they pursued their separate paths as they have continued to do.

Happily, the relationship between the two Companies is now very different. In 1946-7 Mr. Brammall Daniel was Master of the Glovers' Company and he entertained the Master of the Leathersellers at Dinner. It must have been a cordial occasion because the Master of the Leathersellers' Company wrote to say 'it was an added pleasure to visit an ancient guild so intimately connected with our own for over 130 years'.[13] In October 1950 the Leathersellers wrote to enquire if they might be permitted to incorporate the coat of arms of the Glovers' Company in the decorative scheme at Leathersellers' Hall and permission was readily given.[14]

---

[13] Guildhall Library MS 4596 A.
[14] Guildhall Library MS 4591/6. The arms of the Glovers' Company are displayed in Leathersellers' Hall firstly in a scroll in the Assembly Hall where they appear with those of the Pursers and Leathersellers and then in the Reception Room on a handwoven carpet, this time with the Leathersellers', the Saddlers' and Cordwainers' arms.

VII

The Glovers Become a Livery Company

THERE REMAINED one further step for the Company to take. The final stage of development achieved by the Company was the grant of a livery.[1] A request for the right to wear a livery was lodged with the Court of Aldermen in 1680.[2] The Company looked to attend the Lord Mayor in the state and service of the City on solemn occasions, being desirous 'to contribute their uttmost Assistance for supporting the grandeur of this Honourable City'. Perhaps they were wise to wait. By the time the application was made their Charter had been in existence for over 40 years.

The Court of Aldermen appointed a committee to look into the request. The committee reported that the Company was a very ancient company; that they had several considerable citizens as members; that the grant of a livery might be a means of benefit both to the Company and the public in that they would be liable to contribute on all public occasions of the City and, besides, many inferior in antiquity had liveries, but they recommended a grant be made on condition that the Company should solicit no members from other liveries unless they should be translated openly in that Court.

The grant of livery was approved provided that the Company's bye-laws were approved by the Court.[3] The Repertories show the bye-laws or ordinances set out in full in an entry dated 22 March 1680/1.[4] The grant of livery is notable in that it does not limit the number of the livery, although the approved bye-laws allowed the Master to call on members of the Company to take up the livery, the number not to exceed one hundred and twenty. They had to be worth £100 and to pay to the Company £10 in default of accepting their obligation.

The Court of Aldermen seems to have been concerned around this time about the quality of the livery.[5] An order was made confirming that all companies and all members thereof should be under the government of the Court of Aldermen. The Court should order and appoint which companies should have liveries, and members chosen into the livery should first be approved or rejected by the Court which in its discretion might remove any person then or thereafter of the livery.[6] Then, in July 1697, a further order was made. Many were admitted who the Court thought had 'neither estates nor abilities to take the cloathing upon them which proceedings tending not only to ye impoverishment of them and their families but is alsoe at last a charge and burthen to the Companies to which they

---

[1] CLRO REP 90 lists those companies having a livery *de novo* as the Great Twelve and 19 others.
[2] CLRO Companies Box 3.6. From 1560 a company wishing to adopt a livery had first to obtain the approval of the Court of Aldermen. Jones, *The Corporation of London*, p.47.
[3] The Act of Parliament of 1437 mentioned in note 3 to Chapter VI also required that no ordinances should be made except they be approved by the same Justices and governors. An Act of 1504 requires all ordinances made by Fellowships of crafts and misteries to be examined and allowed by the Chancellor and Chief Justices. Jones, *The Corporation of London*, p.47.
[4] CLRO REP 86 and see Appendix IV. These bye-laws still regulate the government of the Company. Later references are given in the modern style of dating.   [5] CLRO REP 92.   [6] ibid.

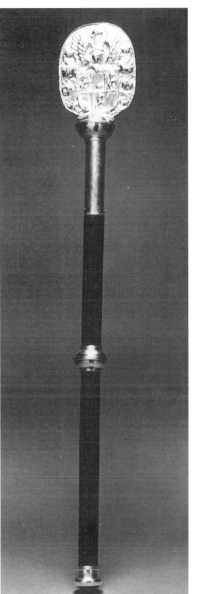

7   Charles II chased tulips two-handled silver porringer, 1669.

8   Charles II silver and ebony mace. The gift of Walter Thomas, 1680.

belong'. It was ordered that those taking the livery of the Twelve Companies should have estates of £1,000 and those taking any other livery should have estates of £500.

From this time onwards (except in the case of the Farriers' Company in 1692) grants of livery were limited to fixed numbers. Examples of such limitations occur in the grants to the Pewterers and the Coachmakers in 1685 and 1687 respectively, and the Loriners and the Glass Sellers, both in 1712. It has been suggested that a possible reason for this practice was the need to keep the number of liverymen entitled to vote at Common Hall within reasonable proportions.

Perhaps the fact that no limit of numbers was stipulated in the grant of livery to the Glovers was a lacuna. About a century later, on 18 April 1774, the members of the Court of the Glovers' Company declared[7] that they were not bound either by the bye-laws of 1680 or the constitution of the City from admitting more than 120 members to the livery. The yeomanry or freemen had considerably increased and several more had been made liverymen and more yeomen would like to take up the livery but were discouraged by the ill-grounded fear that their right of voting at elections would be invalidated under the bye-laws. The Court therefore proceeded to repeal the bye-law limiting the number of liverymen. Thereafter the Company considered the livery unlimited and the City authorities seem to have acquiesced.

The question of numbers does not seem to have recurred again until 1944. At the Corporation of London Record Office is a note from the Glovers' Company[8] to the effect that the Master had received a communication from the Court of Aldermen suggesting that the Company should resign its right to an unlimited livery in exchange for a limit of 250 members. No reasons were given. The Glovers thought that that would reduce their dignity. They were one of 56 such Companies and they drew attention to the resolution of 1774 recently confirmed by the Company. As the bye-laws were submitted for enrolment the annulment was 'out of courtesy' also submitted for enrolment. The Company regarded enrolment as procedural since the power to make, alter and repeal bye-laws was in the Charter. Accordingly they were unwilling to accede to the request and there the matter rested.[8]

Undoubtedly the absence of numerical restriction has been an advantage to the Company which is now one of the largest of the livery companies. At the present time the number of liverymen is 266 and rising.

From 1680 the Company ranked in all respects *pari passu* with the other City companies with the right to elect the Lord Mayor and to join in the ceremonies and celebrations of their liveried brethren.

A few years later, in 1684, a writ of Quo Warranto obliged the City companies to surrender their charters to the Crown so that more acceptable documents administered by more amenable appointees might take their place. It gave the Crown control over both the appointment and removal of officers and assistants and required them to take the Oath of Allegiance and the Oath of Supremacy and make a declaration against the Solemn League and Covenant.[9] Curiously, the Glovers seem to have been overlooked. In any event, in 1688 the companies had their original charters restored.

---

[7]   Guildhall Library MS 4591.
[8]   CLRO Companies Box 10.31. Alongside the note in a different hand the word 'Nonsense' is written in pencil.
[9]   The Oath of Allegiance was in common terms to be faithful and bear true allegiance to the King. The Oath of Supremacy was fashioned as a rebuttal of the Papal authority. In robust terms those taking the oath swore 'from the heart' to abhor, detest and abjure the concept that princes excommunicated could be deposed or murdered by their subjects and affirmed that no foreign prince or prelate had any authority 'within this realm'. The Solemn League and Covenant was made in 1643 between Parliament and the Scots whereby the Scottish army came to the aid of the Parliamentary forces and it was agreed that the two nations would combine to abolish episcopacy and establish a uniform Presbyterian church.

VIII

Internal Controversies and Disputes

T HERE WAS, in fact, a particularly troublesome consequence resulting from the writ of Quo Warranto. Several members of the Court of Assistants were removed from office by virtue of an order of the Privy Council. On 6 November 1688, John Philpott and seven others applied to the Court of Aldermen to be restored to their former position.[1] It was said that the removal had been made on the supposition that the Company had surrendered its charter and obtained a new one empowering the King to turn out any of the Assistants by order. That was not the case. The Charter had not been surrendered. The Court ordered the Master and present members of the Court to readmit the former Assistants.

By the following January nothing had happened. Philpott and his colleagues were obliged to go back to the Court of Aldermen for their further assistance.[2] This time the order was for the Master, Wardens and Assistants of the Glovers' Company to attend the Court of Aldermen and answer for their contempt. How the matter was eventually dealt with does not seem to be recorded but, no doubt, John Philpott and the others were eventually restored to office.

By February 1690[3] the Glovers were driven to petition the Court of Aldermen that the number of their Assistants might be increased. The Charter stipulated that the Court should number 21 members out of which four Wardens were chosen annually. That could not be done unless the number was increased because all the present Assistants had passed the office of Warden. They asked that their number be increased to 31 and that was allowed by the Court of Aldermen.

Around this time it almost seemed as if the Glovers, having resolved their differences with the Leathersellers' Company, were determined to quarrel among themselves.

The Company was faced with a problem in 1667 when William Read, who was chosen to be a Warden, refused either to take office or pay the fine for refusal. He was brought before the Lord Mayor's Court.[4] He was ordered to pay the fine in two half-yearly instalments and to give the Company security for payment.

A few days later,[5] the Lord Mayor heard a dispute between Miss Elizabeth Hytch and John Yates, the glover who employed her. She claimed the sum of £4 10s. 0d. for a year and a half's wages due. Yates counterclaimed for £2 5s. 0d. for money lent to her and for buying necessaries for her. The Lord Mayor ordered Yates to pay Miss Hytch £2 5s. 0d. in full satisfaction for her wages 'And all sutes now depending between them to be withdrawn'. Yates must have indicated dissatisfaction because in another hand is

---

[1] CLRO REP 94.
[2] ibid.
[3] CLRO REP 95.
[4] CLRO Lord Mayor's Waiting Book 3 October 1667.
[5] ibid., 6 October 1667.

added 'The sayd difference being againe heard by his Lordshipp, his Lordshippe did further order that ye sayd Yates doe pay ye said Hytch £2 and noe more And so all differences to cease'.

The Repertories show[6] that in 1674 John Riley made allegation that the Company was acting contrary to the tenure of its Charter through it is not clear how the complaint arose or what its outcome was.

A much more troublesome dispute arose in 1675. Joseph Coles, a member of the Company, was accused by David Jones, whom he had formerly employed as a journeyman, of discharging him without any warning contrary to the Company's ordinances which required the employer to give a fortnight's notice. Jones applied to the Court of Assistants for relief and the Clerk was ordered to give him a certificate which would enable him to get employment until a hearing could be arranged. In due course Mr. Coles appeared before the Court. He was incensed. He was fined for arresting David Jones without the consent of the Company and for uttering scandalous and opprobrious words against the Court. He refused peremptorily either to submit to the Court or pay the fines. It was in these circumstances that the Court of Assistants felt obliged to order him to appear before the Court of Aldermen. The Master, supported by two Wardens and seven Assistants undertook to attend. Mr. Coles was charged with behaving himself contemptuously to the Company, refusing to yield obedience to their ordinances and using irreverent and unbecoming expressions towards them. On his appearance before the Court of Aldermen in the presence of the Master and Wardens he promised his ready submission to the ordinances of the Company in light of which the Court[7] thought proper to reprove Coles for his misbehaviour and admonished him to be more dutiful and conformable to the Company for the future. The Court recommended the Master and Wardens to treat him favourably in respect of several fines imposed upon him for his offence and all other demands which the Company had upon him.

Happily, Mr. Coles submitted and paid his fines. The order of the Court of Aldermen reads:

Sheldon, Mayor.

Jovio Secundo die Decembrio Anoque Caroli sedi etc xxvii

This day Joseph Coles, Cittizen and Glover of London being convened before this Court upon Complaint of the Master, Wardens and Assistants of the Company of Glovers for behaving himselfe contemptuously of the said Company refuseing to yeild obedience to their ordinances and useing irreverent and misbeseeming expressions towards them did here in the presence of the said Master and Wardens declare and promise his ready submission to the orders of the said Company. Whereupon the Court did thinke fitt to reprove the said Coles for his said misbehaviour and admonish him to bee more duty full for ye future And did thinke fitt to recommend it to ye said Master Wardens and Assistants to threate him favourably in respect of several fines by them imposed upon him for his said offence and all other demands which the said Company have upon him.

[6] CLRO REP 79.   [7] CLRO REP 81.

It is evident that Mr. Coles was a hot tempered gentleman.[8] About the same time a fellow Glover, Mr. Peter Hebb, complained that Mr. Coles had abused him in scurrilous language which was afterwards proved by Mr. Baker another Glover. Mr. Coles confessed to saying that Mr. Hebb was 'an old foole and a cheating knave, that he had mortgaged his lease to a leatherseller and that he would have given £100 with his daughter to her portion and give Bond for the same'. Both parties agreed to accept the decision of the Court of Assistants. The Court fined Mr. Coles 3s. 4d and this time he paid it.

In October 1677 Mr. Coles was in trouble again for retaining quarterage collected for the Company's use. He was summoned to appear before the Lord Mayor but there is no record of his doing so and the matter must have been resolved. In April 1678 he was fined for not attending the Master on being lawfully summoned to accompany him on undertaking the Quarter Search, i.e. the search to check materials and workmanship. However, it is possible to conclude this passage concerning Mr. Coles on a happier note. It is much to his credit that he was one of 26 members of the Court who in 1678 each contributed £2 towards furnishing the Hall. He evidently bore no grudges and could be generously disposed.

An altogether more serious matter was the complaint[9] by John Churchill and several other Assistants against the Master, Mr. Isaac Shard, the Wardens and other Assistants of the Company. A long and detailed indictment of the alleged transgressions of Mr. Shard and the others has survived and is set out in Appendix V. It makes clear that the facts giving rise to the dispute went back for a number of years and that they preceded the appointment of John Wildman as clerk in January 1693. The supposed malpractices included the calling of courts in coffee houses, ale houses and taverns instead of in the Hall. Some of these courts might be termed private meetings and were held almost daily. As a result the Company's records ceased to be properly kept, wrongful bindings of apprentices and granting of freedoms were allowed, the Company's money was squandered and the Company impoverished. In 1694 the Court of Assistants had called to account the then Master, Mr. Shutt, and the Renter Warden and finding their management so irregular, the Master not even being a freeman of London, they removed them. Mr. Farding, the Master in 1694, attempted to rectify matters by holding regular monthly courts and the Clerk was given custody of the Company's books and papers. However, in 1696, when Mr. Hobday was Master and in 1698, Mr. Jones being Master, they and their Renter Wardens ignored the resolutions made in Mr. Farding's day and began to hold private courts again and misapplied the Company's funds. John Wildman, the Clerk, tried to do his duty but drew down the enmity of those who wished to be free of any rules and they refused to employ him about the Company's business.

That was how matters stood when Mr. Shard was made Master in 1699. Hitherto he had always seemed zealous in opposing abuses but as soon as he was appointed Master he said he was not going to be bound by any restraints and would hold courts as often as he wished. He took in his own hands £50 of the Company's money which should have been under the Renter Warden's control and took from the Clerk the Company's books

---

[8]   Subsequent references to Mr. Coles are taken from the Company's Minute book for 1675 to 1679 (Guildhall Library MS 4591).
[9]   CLRO Companies Box 3.6 and CLRO REP 104.

and records. He attempted to have the earlier order requiring only monthly courts repealed and endeavoured to hold courts whenever he wished despite the fact that most Assistants opposed that practice. He would have no monthly courts. Quite irregularly, he appointed a Mr. East to act as clerk. He refused to allow John Wildman to officiate and at a particular court told him to withdraw. When some of the Assistants protested the Master and 'his Accomplices did thereupon Ruffle and Assault some of the Assistants then present' and assaulted Mr. Wildman 'to the hazzard of his life' for which assault the Master had been indicted before a Grand Jury. The Master had refused to refer these differences with the Complainants to the Court of Aldermen. The Complainants therefore asked the Court to deprive the Master and his (named) associates of their 'Honours Offices and Places and all those Franchises and privileges which in common with other citizens they were entitled to'.

The complaint came before the Court of Aldermen on 12 July 1700,[10] and after two adjournments John Chambers and Richard Martin, two of the Assistants, petitioned the Court that the Lord Mayor himself should consent to attend their Election Day Court in September to preside there 'to settle their differences and prevent any disorders'. This the Court agreed to recommend.

Then in October 1700 Mr. Shard appeared before the Court of Aldermen.[11] It is clear that the Election Day Court had been an unhappy occasion. The Court debated 'the affronts and contempts offered and done to the Right Honourable the Lord Mayor and this Court by the said Shard and part of the Wardens and Assistants of the same (Company of Glovers)'. It was ordered that no more courts or proceedings should be held by the Glovers' Company until the committee appointed by the Court of Aldermen to look into the affronts given to the Lord Mayor and the events giving rise to the complaints made by Churchill and others had reported their findings. Furthermore Mr. East should be precluded from officiating as Clerk until further order and Shard and his allies should attend before the committee when required. The Town Clerk was to place the alleged contempts before the Recorder and the Common Sergeant for their opinions.

In April 1701 Mr. Martin, a member of the Glovers' Company, complained to the Court of Aldermen[12] that several persons had improperly been made free of the Company and that he and several others who, in obedience of the Court's orders, had stayed away from (domestic) courts, were being fined for their absence. As customary, a committee was appointed to look into the matter. Further complaints were lodged showing that the 'undue and refractory practices' of Mr. Shard and his allies continued and Mr. Wildman, the Clerk, was told to instruct the Recorder and the Common Sergeant with full details of the proceedings relating to the Company.[13]

How it all ended is not clear but Mr. Shard must have continued to prosper. In a 'Poll of the liverymen of the City of London' published in 1710[14] he is described as Sir Isaac Shard.

[10] CLRO REP 104.
[11] ibid.
[12] CLRO REP 105.
[13] ibid.
[14] In the writer's possession.

Not much seems to have gone right for the Glovers' Company about this time. In January 1702,[15] Thomas Hatch came before the Court of Aldermen to petition for his freedom. It appeared to the Court that there had been

> very irregular and notorious Practices frequently done and committed in the Glovers' Company by contriving and procuring several persons to be unduly bound to Freemen and serving Forreigners their whole Apprenticeshipps and then presenting them to the Chamberlains as if they had duely served such Freemen to whom they were so bound as aforesaid whereby many have been fraudulently made free of this City to the great prejudice thereof.

A committee was appointed to investigate the matter but there is no indication that any action was taken.

Trouble of a rather different kind was evident two years later. In September 1704[16] the Girdlers, the Scriveners and the Glovers were summoned to attend the Court of Aldermen to show cause why they did not obey the precepts directed to them 'touching her Majesties Reception into this City in her passage to St. Pauls Church upon Thursday next'.

Evidently a certain amount of laxity among the companies was becoming evident. Some years later in October 1737[17] the Court of Aldermen took

> notice that of late years several of the Livery Companies of this City have neglected to give their attendance on the new Lord Mayor on the day he goes to Westminster to be sworn and that several others who do go out on that day do not continue in their stands till his Lordship's return from Westminster in contempt of the antient and laudable custom of this City and to the dishonour of the government thereof. The Court doth therefore strictly require and enjoyn the Masters and Wardens of the several livery Companies of this City to take especial care that all their members do attend on the next Lord Mayor's day in their livery gowns at their proper stands which are to be set out by Mr. George Dance Clerk of this City's Works and that they do not remove from the said stands till after his Lordship's return from Westminster to Guildhall to Dinner. The Court having given directions that particular notice be taken of such Companies who shall offend in any of the premises that they may be proceeded against for such their neglect and contempt according to the laws and customs of this City. And it is ordered that copys hereof be forthwith printed and sent to the Masters and Wardens of the several livery Companies of this City that they may not plead ignorance thereof.

---

[15] CLRO REP 107.   [16] CLRO REP 108.   [17] CLRO REP 141.

IX

The Control of the Craft is Enforced

THE 18TH CENTURY was a time when commerce and industry expanded greatly. It witnessed the birth of the industrial revolution and it witnessed also the passing of the last vestiges of the medieval trade guild. The time came when the livery companies were no longer able and they no longer sought to control the practice of the crafts they represented.

The opposition to the doctrine supporting restraint of trade is not new. The custom of London was itself a liberal tradition where a freeman could pursue whatever trade or business he wished irrespective of the company to which he belonged, but by the 18th century the burgeoning population and the growth of manufacture ensured that the companies could no longer enforce ordinances which had been seen as appropriate in simpler times, and as the century proceeded the Court of Aldermen was involved less and less in aiding the enforcement of company regulations.[1]

The mood was the same all over the country. Although it is not strictly relevant to the practice of the City it is interesting to see that the provincial boroughs were facing not dissimilar problems. In 1721 there was a landmark case at Kingston-on-Thames.[2] Sir Robert Raymond of counsel advised the Borough that the Corporation of Kingston would not be able to force a trader to take his freedom before practising his trade unless it was able to rely on ancient custom. Counsel had known of several attempts to enforce such a bye-law but they never succeeded except in London, where customs were confirmed by Act of Parliament and the custom of the City excluding foreigners from trading unless they were free was upheld in no other corporation whatever.

All over the country provincial companies were facing similar problems to those affecting the victuallers of Kingston. They had to change and adapt to new circumstances.

In the City the effect on many of the minor companies seems to have been to deprive them of an essential element of their *raison d'etre*; the regulation and enforcement of trading standards. In later years they were in large part to take up again their concerns with training and with the achievement of excellence in the quality of the materials used or the arts which they represented, but for a time, indeed for a substantial period of time, they lapsed into an apparent state of apathy. By 1756 no more than eight per cent of the Glovers' Company were said to practise the craft.[3] In part, of course, the overall decline was caused by the decline of the gloving industry within the City but the minutes of the Company from about 1773 reveal none of the urgency to rule and control the industry which had so engrossed the Company a century earlier.

---

[1] Unwin, *The Gilds and Companies*, p.344.   [2] BL Lansdowne MS 226.
[3] J.R. Kellett, *The Economic History Review*, April 1958.

It is instructive to look again at how strongly and how faithfully and for how long the members of the Glovers' Company had struggled to give effective government to their craft, that constant issue which had exercised the minds of those guiding the Company from the time of the first stirrings of revolt within the ranks of the Leathersellers. We have seen that a recurring concern of the Glovers and the other handicraft companies up to this time was to obtain and retain control of all the workers of their craft within the City and its environs. Thereby they would be able to maintain proper standards of workmanship and materials. They would also be able to ensure that the apprentice system was not abused. A direct consequence of the policy was the preservation of the status of the master craftsman. Ideally, the policy involved the transfer of the working craftsman to the company of the craft he practised. In that way he came under the direct control of the Master and Wardens through the company's bye-laws. So long as the craftsman was free in another company it was obviously difficult to control his actions.

The Statute of Apprentices passed in 1563 required an apprentice to engage in the trade or craft he had been taught but that requirement seems never to have been regularly enforced and from the point of view of the handicraft companies the situation was not helped by the custom of London giving freemen liberty to trade as they wished. There was some improvement of the craftsmen's position in 1634 when a committee of the Court of Aldermen decided[4] that the custom of London only applied to 'merchandizing and trades' and not to the craft companies, and from about this time the Court seems to have been amenable on occasion to requests from those companies for translations of their fellows from other companies.

The Glovers' Company was at pains to make clear to the Court of Aldermen when having its Charter recorded and again when applying for the livery that it did not seek to incommode or undermine other companies by making requests for the translation of unwilling glovers. That would have been to invite controversy and while, on occasions, the City was sympathetic to requests where there were sound underlying reasons, consent for translation of freemen was granted sparingly. However, from the time of the Commonwealth it seems to have become easier to promote such translations with the City's concurrence.[5] As noted earlier, in 1613 the Leathersellers' Company acting on behalf of the working glovers had obtained the City's approval to the binding of apprentices of 'foreign' working glovers to members of the Company so that in due course they might be admitted to the freedom of the Company and thereby brought under control. In 1631 the Leathersellers' Company again successfully petitioned the Court of Aldermen on behalf of the glovers that the apprentices of all working glovers whether free or foreign be bound to a member of the Company that they might in due course be free thereof.[6]

The Journals of the Court of Common Council show that in July 1651[7] a committee of the Court considered a petition lodged by the Glovers' Company praying that all apprentices taken by anyone and of whatever Company using the glovers' craft should be bound at Glovers' Hall and made free of the Glovers' Company, and that a certain number

[4] CLRO REP 48.
[6] CLRO REP 45.
[5] Unwin, *The Gilds and Companies*, p.343.
[7] CLRO JOR 41x.

of 'foreign' glovers should be admitted to the freedom of the City and the Company by redemption 'for the better rule and government thereof'.

As to the first request (dealing with apprentices), the Court found precedents in earlier Mayoralties in favour of the Glaziers and the Painter Stainers, and as to the request for admission of 'foreign' glovers, there were earlier precedents in favour of the Weavers and the Brewers which would support it. The Weavers and Brewers had each applied for 30 'foreigners' to be introduced into their Companies by redemption but the Glovers, more modestly, only applied for 12, which the committee thought very reasonable and recommended be accepted.

The Glovers had complained that there were a number of freemen of the City practising the art of glove making who had never been apprenticed in the trade and were free of other companies. Such people had taken apprentices of their own, more than the Company of Glovers would allow, 'to the pestering and filling this City with men of that facultie and profession to the great prejudice and hinderance of the Freemen of the Company of Glovers by reason whereof much bad and deceiptfull workemanship is daiely practised', mainly because those men were not subject to the ordinances of the Glovers.

The committee recommended that all freemen using the art of glove making or of a working glover within the City should, in time, be brought within the ranks of the Glovers' Company. All those actually practising the craft, despite the fact that they might be freemen of other companies, should be subject to the survey and search of the Master and Wardens of the Glovers' Company and subject to its ordinances. If any glover free of another company took an apprentice he must within one month present the apprentice to the Master and Wardens of the Glovers' Company to be bound to one of them. Thereafter the apprentice would be set over before the Chamberlain to his own master to complete his term. On completion of that term the apprentice would be made free of the Glovers' Company. If that injunction was broken the committee recommended that a penalty of £20 be imposed on the offending glover. The penalty should be recoverable as a simple debt and 'no wager of lawe shalbe admitted or allowed for the defence'. To encourage the Glovers' Company to prosecute offenders they were to receive half of any fines imposed.

Other companies were quick to follow the lead of the Glovers. Within the next decade no less than 14 other companies including the Blacksmiths, the Turners, the Weavers and the Feltmakers were to promote similar regulations for the government of apprentices.

A few years after the Common Council had made this recommendation, which was accepted, a further problem arose. The Chamberlain felt unauthorised from making apprentices of the kind referred to free in the Company of Glovers on completion of their term as that was not mentioned in the order made. Accordingly the Glovers brought the matter before the Court of Aldermen and in January 1654[8] the Court, acknowledging that the purpose of the Common Council's decision was to reduce all working glovers to membership of the Company of Glovers for the better government of the craft,

---

8   CLRO REP 63.

specifically directed the Chamberlain to make free by birth or service respectively as the case required the sons and apprentices of freemen occupying the craft of glover and bound since, the earlier order notwithstanding, the father or master, being glover by trade, was free of another Company 'soe as such Apprentice of such Freeman or Freemen shall demand and desire the same'.

Such measures were designed to bring under the control of the Glovers' Company new members of the craft as they took up the freedom. They did not affect those practitioners who were already free of other companies. The translation of members from one company to another was a more sensitive issue. Nevertheless during the latter half of the 17th century and the first half of the 18th century Acts of Common Council were passed with a view to making membership of the lesser companies coincident with the membership of the trades they represented. The practice was for six members of each company to attend before the Chamberlain with the freeman concerned to signify their consent to his translation. There are several instances in the Company's records and the City Repertories of such proceedings. The Court of Aldermen had the power to grant the freedom of a company to an applicant without apparently joining that company as a party to the proceedings. For example, John Langley, an apprentice glover, asked the Court to admit him to the freedom of that Company in September 1698. He explained that he had served five years of his term and that his master had died and his master's executors had remitted the balance of the period of his service. He was admitted by redemption to the Company of Glovers on payment to the Chamberlain of the quite substantial sum of £5.[9]

About this time it was accepted practice to give those who served the City the right to grant the freedom to their nominees by way of redemption as a reward for their services. No doubt it also served to help the City's finances. The Repertories show that in 1694[10] 'for the incouragement of several officers of the City in the execution of their offices the Court granted for their benefit several freeman's rooms. None to be disposed of until those granted in Sir John Fleet's Mayoralty bee sold.' The Swordbearer had an annual grant of three under an order of 26 November 1706. The usual price paid for a freedom was £25.[11]

It became quite common to see an official like the Common Cryer or the Clerk to the Commissioner of Sewers present to the Court persons whom he wished to be made free in this way. Several were made free of the Glovers' Company. In 1697[12] Ralph Lawrence was presented as the first of three granted during the Mayoralty of Sir John Houblon to the Clerk to the Commissioner of Sewers. He had to pay £2 6s. 8d. to the Chamberlain. Similarly, James Seignioret, the first of two granted to the Clerk of Works in the Mayoralty of Sir Thomas Lane,[13] was admitted to the Glovers' Company and there were others. In 1713 when three names were before it the Court exercised its discretion to allocate the applicants to the Company of Leathersellers, the Company of Weavers and the Company of Glovers respectively. They each paid a fee of £2 6s. 8d. to the

---

[9] CLRO REP 102.
[10] CLRO REP 98 and see CLRO REP 118 where a freedom was ordered (1 December 1713) to be sold for the infirm son of a former Lord Mayor.   [11] CLRO REP 101.   [12] ibid.
[13] ibid.

Chamberlain.[14] Indeed, the Lord Mayor himself had the prerogative of sale, and on 7 October 1697 he presented to the Court Giles Shoote as one due to his lordship in the right of his late lady. Shoote was ordered to be admitted into the Glovers' Company.[15]

Towards the middle of the 18th century there seem to have been several instances where the Glovers themselves had to translate members, often to the Innholders. In 1734, Thomas Clark,[16] in 1735 Samuel Purt,[17] in 1742 John Turton,[18] in 1743 James Cooper[19] and in 1746 John Star[20] were translated from the Glovers to the Innholders. In each case the freeman concerned kept an inn within the City. In 1706 there had been the special case of Samuel Sheldon.[21] He had been instructed by the Glovers' Company to serve as a Steward on Lord Mayor's Day that year. This was regarded as an onerous office and there are many instances of freemen being prepared to pay a fine to the Company rather than serve. The question for the Court of Aldermen was whether Sheldon, on serving as Steward for the Glovers, would be liable to serve as Steward for the Innholders on translation to that Company. The Court held that he would not. Apparently once was enough.

In 1736 Daniel Smith,[22] a member of the Glovers' Company who was an innholder by trade, was brought before the Court of Aldermen. It was found that he had become a Glover knowing full well that by an Act of the Common Council made in May 1663 he should have been admitted to the Innholders' Company at the instance of that Company. He had paid the Glovers £14 so as to be exempt from all offices in the Company. The question was whether, on translation, he should be exempt from office in the Innholders' Company. He was ordered to be translated and to be subject to serve the several offices of the Innholders.

Of course the Innholders' Company was not the only company which sought to obtain translations from the Glovers. In 1739 Thomas White was translated to the Stationers.[23] In 1744 John Grant was translated to the Soapmakers' Company[24] and in 1747 Thomas Conyers, an apothecary, was translated to that Company.[25]

A translation of a different kind was made on 13 September 1737[26] when, by consent of six Glovers and six Grocers, Sir John Barnard Knight, Alderman and Glover, was translated to the Grocers' Company. Sir John was Lord Mayor in that year.

The efforts of the Glovers' Company and other craft companies to maintain direct control over those practising their craft within the City were, however, seen in time to be of little value. As the 18th century progressed translations of craftsmen to their parent company became of transitory importance in an expanding economy. By the time of the Municipal Corporations Report in 1837 only the Company of Carmen was composed of men following the occupation of the company of which they were members.

---

[14] CLRO REP 118.   [15] CLRO REP 101.   [16] CLRO REP 140.
[17] ibid.   [18] CLRO REP 141.   [19] CLRO REP 148.
[20] CLRO REP 150.   [21] CLRO REP 111.   [22] CLRO REP 140.
[23] CLRO REP 143.   [24] CLRO REP 148.   [25] CLRO REP 151.
[26] CLRO REP 141.

X

The Company at Work

THE ARCHIVES OF the Glovers' Company are lodged at the Guildhall Library. Sadly, nothing prior to the 17th century has survived and, apart from a copy of the Charter of Charles I and a copy of the ordinances of 1681, there is not a great deal from the next 100 years.[1] However, the minutes of the Court of Assistants for the period 1675-9 are there[2] and, together with some apprentice bindings,[3] they give us a glimpse of the workings of the Company at a time when the traditional activities of a livery company, in this case *working* glovers and leatherdressers, were still the major concern of those involved.

In an earlier chapter a number of disputes and disagreements were described, some even involving the Master himself and all suggesting an absence of harmony and direction from those in authority, but probably the Glovers were not much different from other livery companies who were not exempt from either trade or personal factions or quarrels. Certainly much of the content of the minutes shows that the business of the Court was generally of a routine nature and it is useful to analyse the records of that time to try to obtain an understanding of what the Company actually did and what the concerns of its members were.

By the time the minutes open in 1675 the Company was already in possession of a hall.[4] It was situated, appropriately, not far from New Church Haw without Aldersgate. Glovers' Hall was at the south end of Glovers' Hall Court, off Beech Lane in Cripplegate Ward Without, according to Ogilby and Morgan's Map of London 1676. *A Topographical Dictionary of London* by James Elmes published in 1831 is rather more specific. It describes Glovers' Hall Court as being 'about seven houses on the left from White Cross Street. In this court was the ancient hall of the Glovers' Company who now transact their business at a tavern.' Beech Street connected Barbican and Chiswell Street, lying between Red Cross Street and White Cross Street, and Beech Lane was situate about the middle of the south side of Beech Street.

There are several references to the Hall and to improvements to be carried out there.[5] The building was held on lease and on 12 September 1678 the Court of Assistants

---

[1] The Company of Glovers is greatly indebted to Theophilus Charles Noble, a member of the Company of Ironmongers, and to the Guildhall Library for the preservation of much of its archive. Mr. Noble was a true citizen of London and wrote extensively about a variety of subjects including the Spanish Armada, Temple Bar, The Mayoralty, Crystal Palace and St Bartholomew's Hospital. He was an avid collector and after his death there was a two-day sale of his collected works on typography, genealogy, heraldry, etc., including some livery company records. The Corporation of London made a number of purchases. The material relating to the Glovers' Company acquired by the Guildhall Library from Mr. Noble's estate amounts to almost one third of the Glovers' archive. The Guildhall Library still maintains its 'Noble Collection' and the curious may see the extent of his interest by examining the sale catalogue preserved there.
[2] Guildhall Library MS 4591.   [3] Guildhall Library MS 2918.
[4] For an account of the Hall see Appendix VI.   [5] Guildhall Library MS 4591.

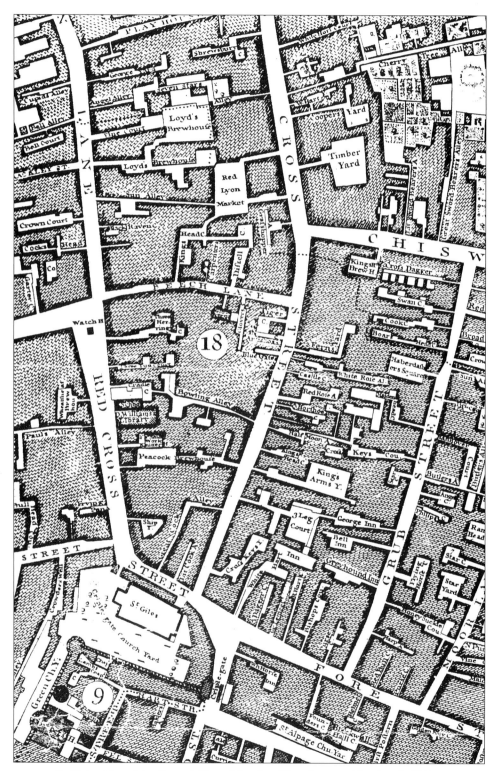

9   Extract from John Rocque's Plan of London, Westminster and Southwark, 1746.

takeing into their consideration the short time they have to come in their lease of their
Hall did order and appoint those persons under named to meet with Mr. Hockenhull next
Monday at eleaven o'clock to treate with him about the takeing of a lease of the present
Hall or such other conveniences as may be fitt for them and that the said persons make
their report to the Company next Court Day of such their proceeding.

The negotiations must have been successful because on 7 October it was ordered that a
lease of the Hall and premises 'bee taken of Mr. Hockenhull for 99 years of the lands
Mr. Hockenhull have power to grant the same att the yearely rent of £20 in which lease
itt is agreed shall bee incerted a covenant for the Company', and on 14 October it was
ordered that the engrossment of the lease should be sealed by the Master and Wardens.

At the same time it was ordered that Mr. Draper, the Company's Clerk, who had the
use of £100, the Company's money, at interest, should pay the money to the Renter Warden
in two equal instalments at intervals of three and six months. When it was received by the
Renter Warden it 'shall bee laid out and expended in building of the new intended Parlour
or Roome according to the Covenants of the Company's lease with Mr. Hockenhull and
to noe other use whatsoever'. A committee was appointed to arrange for someone to
build the parlour and also to 'demise or lett the House of Reynold Sutton now the
Companyes for such time as they shall think fit'.

It was soon found that the parlour was going to cost more than £100 to build and in
November it was ordered that the committee should negotiate the loan of a sum of
money not to exceed £100 at six per cent interest. In May 1679 it was decided that the
parlour 'which is now building' should be wainscotted seven feet high round the walls.
Perhaps the committee did not need to negotiate a loan of £100 because by 27 July
members of the Company undertook to lend the Company £2 each towards furnishing
the Hall and it was ordered that 'the great hall shall be white washed and coloured over
and well seized and layd in good stone colour five foote high'.

The final reference to the Hall shows that it continued to be a source of expense.
The sum of £60 was borrowed to enable the payment of accounts. On the other hand it
is interesting to note that, even at this time, the use of Company Halls was shared.
Throughout the period covered by the minutes the Cardmakers occasionally used the
Hall, paying 5s. for the privilege.

There are constant references in the Minute Book to the Company's ordinances.[6]
Nowadays, of course, ordinances scarcely impinge upon the lives of liverymen but in the
closing years of the 17th century they were of everyday importance and every freeman
and liveryman must have been aware of their effect.

Mr. Francis Aldwin was Master at the first meeting recorded on 27 September 1675.
Two new apprenticeships were registered for which the Company received a fee. Both
show that, then as now, the capital city exercised a powerful influence over young people
seeking to make their way in the world. John Greene of Lemster (Leominster) in
Herefordshire and John Webb of Evill (?Yeovil) in Somerset were each bound apprentice

---

6   Unless otherwise stated, references in this chapter are taken from the Company's Minute books, see Guildhall Library MS 4591.

for seven years.[7] Courts were held monthly and the following month Margaret Barber was apprenticed. Judith Durham, Elizabeth Clifford and Elizabeth Dakin were admitted as journeywomen, each having completed a full apprenticeship. William Willoughby, who came from Stafford, was able to produce a certificate showing that he had completed an apprenticeship and he too was admitted a journeyman. There are numerous similar entries, all of which attracted a fee varying from 2s. 6d. to 6s. 8d. and then there is an entry of a fine. Mr. Conyers was fined £2 for employing 'unlawful' workers contrary to the ordinances. Presumably he was employing journeymen who had not completed an apprenticeship or for whatever reason were not freemen of the Company.

In the following year Arthur Evans was admitted a master for which he had to pay £5. Then Elizabeth Yeoman was admitted a mistress. She seems to have paid only £1 and both were allowed to pay by instalments. Women figure quite prominently in the minutes either as apprentices or journeywomen and, just occasionally, as mistresses in their own right, a position they were allowed to hold during widowhood or while unmarried.

During the period covered by the Minute Book almost all the freemen admitted to the Company arrived by way of servitude, having completed an apprenticeship and that, of course, included the journeymen and women. The alternative avenues of patrimony and redemption are generally absent but there is an instance of a man paying the quite considerable sum of £5 to be admitted by redemption and Abraham Laywood produced a copy of his father's freedom entered in the 'Booke of Freedoms at Guildhall marked :G:' and was admitted and sworn a freeman. Then there are the young men who were admitted freemen without payment of any fee. Perhaps they were orphans or apprentices who had served their time in Bridewell.[8]

Throughout the period there was a steady stream of apprentices being bound to members of the Company and there are one or two unusual names, particularly among the girls. Names which occur are Grisley Cooley, Bethniel Blythe, Comfort Tovey, Isham Randolph, Hezekial Farmer, Sipio Kinsey and Olburtis Skinner.

Freemen and liverymen being master glovers paid the same quarterage. They paid 8d. each quarter in April, July, October and January and journeymen paid 4d. which the master was responsible for paying over. Mr. Gunter seems to have been a substantial master at this time. In 1675 he was paying for 17 journeymen and women. Under the ordinances it was the duty of the Wardens to collect the money. It cannot have been an easy task. They each seem to have been responsible for a particular district which would make for a more orderly collection and perhaps such districts were also identified as separate areas for search purposes. At any rate in 1678 Mr. Farding was responsible for Westminster Search, Mr. Gibson for White Cross Search, Mr. Masters for Shoreditch

---

[7] The author was particularly gratified to find that on 20 August 1677 'Robert Swan, sonne of Christopher Swan, late of Richmond in the County of Yorke, Fellmonger, deced, was bound to John Degg citizen and glover of London for seaven yeares'.

[8] In 1553 Edward VI gave the Mayor, commonalty and citizens his house in Bridewell for a workhouse for poor and idle persons. It became a house of correction for unruly apprentices and vagrants and was demolished in 1863. An unruly apprentice could be committed from the Chamberlain's Court to Bridewell for a period of up to three months and at one time apprentices were allowed to mingle with vagrants and other prisoners there. Segregation of apprentices in sound-proofed cells was arranged in 1800 and when Bridewell prison was closed and reconstituted as King Edward's School the Corporation insisted that some provision should continue to be made for recalcitrant apprentices. Three (later reduced to two) rooms were set aside for them and by custom a copy of *Pilgrim's Progress* was placed in each room. The last apprentice detained there was in 1916. Jones, *The Corporation of London*, pp.91 and 218.

Search and Mr. Rogers for Southwark Search. In October 1677 the Company received 174 payments at the rate of 4d., 59 at the rate of 8d. and five others of varying amounts. Even so, in July 1676 four freemen were fined for refusing to pay.

In the same year Humphrey Jones was fined for not appearing before the Court of Assistants when summoned to do so contrary to the ordinances, and Samuel Bradford was fined £4 for binding four apprentices to him at a scrivener's office and not presenting them to the Company to be there bound. It was the task of the Clerk to prepare the Apprenticeship Indenture for which he and the Beadle each received a fee so no doubt they had cause to be displeased. In January 1678 three journeymen were fined according to the ordinances for cutting leather and working as if masters though not having been admitted masters by the Company.

That the search was still being carried out was evidenced by the fine imposed on Mr. Coles for failing to accompany the Master when he was carrying out that duty and in 1679 Mr. Hetherington was given leave by the Court of Assistants to sue Mr. Francis, a fellow Glover, for abusing him on the search by way of an assault.

Generally during this brief period the Court was well attended. At the first meeting Mr. Aldwin was supported by three Wardens and 14 Assistants. However, when members of the Court did not attend they were not readily excused. In October 1678 no less than 19 Assistants, including the last Master, were fined for not attending, it being Quarter Day. In later Minute Books in the next century Courts often seem to have been poorly attended. There was from time to time a marked reluctance shown to acceptance of office. In March 1676 it was ordered that writs be issued in the Court of Exchequer against all persons who had been lawfully summoned by the Court of Assistants to appear and had failed to do so. Mr. Cantrell was one of those affected by the order. He had been summoned to be sworn in as an Assistant but was absent. Later he appeared and put forward various reasons why he should be excused from office. The Court thought they were not sufficiently weighty and told him he must serve. Accordingly he was sworn in as an Assistant. This was not an isolated instance. Quite often the Company had difficulty in filling vacancies on the Court perhaps because of the need to pay the fine on admittance or because of the time and effort involved in carrying out the duties.

Election Day was 8 September and in 1676 an order was made by the Court

> that from henceforth for ever all and every the Assistants of this Company which now are or hereafter shall be Assistants thereof shall be exempted and discharged from paying any quarteridge to the Company. It is also ordered that such persons as are Assistants of the Company and have dishonoured the Company shall be discharged from being Assistants thereof and thereupon. Mr. Holt and Mr. Bishe were accordingly discharged.
>
> It is also ordered that such of the Assistants of the Company that have not appeared at Court according to their summons should be discharged from being Assistants and thereupon Mr. Latimer and Mr. Gunter were discharged.

The practice at that time was to put forward three nominations, including the outgoing Master, for the person to serve as Master and two nominations for each of the Wardens.

There are several references to the duties of the Clerk and the Beadle and since such duties have changed over the years it is useful to examine what they were called upon to do. The Clerk would, of course, attend meetings of the Court and be responsible for arranging the business to be conducted. He would be responsible for the records of the Company, not merely for the writing of the minutes but for maintaining records of apprentices, members and officers, and quarterage fees, general financial records and records of administration.

In this particular period the Clerk seems to have had control, at least for a time, of the Company's money. It has been mentioned earlier that the Clerk, Mr. Draper, had the use of £100 of the Company's money at six per cent interest and there are other entries showing that he held it under the general direction of the Court.

Occasionally he would be involved in Parliamentary affairs or in instructing an attorney or counsel to defend the Company's interest. In March 1677 it was ordered that 30 shillings be paid to the Clerk which he paid to Mr. Cole, the Clerk of the Weavers Company, and that he should be allowed such charges as he should be at in attending Parliament and, a little later, it was ordered that the money paid out in and about 'making a defence against a bill exhibited by foreigners against the liberties and privileges of freemen shall be allowed and paid by the Company'. Then in October 1679 counsel and an attorney or solicitor were to be instructed to defend an information brought against the Company by the King.

Above all the Clerk was the Company's link with the City and the other livery companies and the multitude of activities they engendered.

The Beadle on the other hand seems to have been the link between the Master and the Wardens and Court of Assistants and the freemen, liverymen and apprentices. At this time he himself would be a freeman of the Company and he had an assistant who was also a freeman.

One of the first entries in the Minute Book relates to the appointment of David Nichols as under-Beadle to help William Hall. Later his wage was fixed at £5 for the year. Half of that sum was to be deducted from the salary of £10 paid to William Hall and half from the Company's funds. He was told that it was his duty, with or without the Beadle, to summon Courts and find out where members lived and accompany the searchers on their visitations and attend at the Hall every Court day. As an indication of the difficulties surrounding the collection of quarterage, he was also told that he would be allowed 3d. in the shilling for all arrears of quarterage of journeymen not gathered by the Wardens in their several divisions and collected by him.

Probably the most unpopular office within the Company and the most difficult to fill was that of Steward.

The ordinances provide

> And every person that shall be elected and chosen Steward of the said Company being a Member of the said Company (there being fower yearely to be chosen by the Master Wardens and Assistants into the office of Stewards, who are to make a Feast or diner with wine musicke and attendants on the Lord Maior's Day as is accustomed by severall other Companies. And to receive their Bill of Fare to be provided on such Occation from the said Master Wardens and Assistants) And being so Chosen shall refuse to take upon him and hold the said Office he shall for his refusall and contempt therein forfeit and pay to the use of the said Company the summe of Tenne pounds of lawfull English money

unless the person chosen to the said office of a Steward shall take his Corporall Oath before the Lord Maior of this Citty for the time being that he is not worth in Cleare Estate One hundred pounds in which case the person that shall take the said Oath shall be excused for that present Yeare from holding the said Office of Steward.

The Minute Books contain frequent refusals of the office and attempts to evade responsibility for payment of the fine. In November 1675 Mr. Blaze Allen appeared before the Court of Assistants having put the Company to the expense of suing him for the recovery of a fine of (only) £2 imposed on him for refusing to take office. He appeared and paid the fine and was excused from paying the Court costs.

On acceptance of his duties the Steward was required to make a declaration. That of Thomas Corwell has survived. He wrote:

I Thomas Corwell doe hereby promise and oblige myselfe to the Company of Glovers London to hold as Steward of the said Company with such other person or persons as they shall appointe to provide a dinner for them and their wives on such a day as they shall appointe and according to the Bill of Fare to be given by the Company.

The Court had ordered that

letters be sent to Thomas Corwell and Mr. Simon King, Stewards elected and chosen for the present yeare of the Company of Glovers London that they take care to provide their dinner and feast to bee kept at Glovers' Hall London on Thursday the 29th of this instant month August according to a bill of fare ordered by the Master Wardens Assistants and Fellowship of the said Company as heretoforth hath been accustomed in that behalfe.

Ordered that att the same feast or dinner of the Stewards to bee kept this yeare that the Company shall not contribute pay or beare any part or charge towards the said feast but that itt shall bee wholly borne and paid att the charge of the said Stewards.

Not even the members of the Court of Assistants were exempt from anxiety. Mr. Rutter and Mr. Farding on being chosen Assistants paid their fines of £3 but simultaneously they were chosen to be Stewards. The Court was merciful. The two men tendered fines of £6 13s. 4d. but the Court thought fit to return to each of them £4 13s. 4d. and 'they are hereby discharged of and from the office of Steward for ever in this Company of Glovers'.

The livery received notice of feasts by way of a 'Stewards Ticquett' delivered presumably by the Beadle or under-Beadle. In 1679 a ticket read:

Sr
You are desired by ye Stewards hereunder named to dine with ye Master Wardens and Assistants of ye Company of Glovers att Glovers Hall in Beach Lane London on Thursday the one and twentieth day of August 1679 at twelve of the clock exactly and to bring this ticquett a long with you for y'r admittance.

David Peersin)		(Phillip Seale
)	Stewards	(
Henry Saunders)		(Thomas Corwen

There are also a few entries which enliven the routine of business. On 7 February 1675 it was recorded that

10   Pair of William and Mary octagonal base pillar candlesticks, 1688-90.

11   Two James II large dome-top tankards and covers, 1685 and 1686.

upon the attestation of Mr. John Dagg, Mr. Hugh Hellres and Mr. Robert Bidle citizens and glovers of London that Mr. William Farrell glover did serve as an apprentice the full terme of seaven years with one Sampson Henley citizen and glover of London who being a Constable and Instrumentall in suppressing the Fifth Monarchy Men was killed. Afterwards in the time of the late conflagration in London the apprentice's Indentures were burned the Indentures being lost and the apprentice deprived of his Master's testimony for his service. And the Court being very well satisfied that the said William Farrell did serve the full terme of his apprenticeship doe think fit and order that the truth thereof be testified to Mr. Thomas Player Chamberlain of the City of London by certificate under the Clerk's hand which he is hereby ordered to make and deliver accordingly.

The Fifth Monarchy Men believed that the second coming of Christ was at hand and that Christians had a duty to be ready to assist in establishing his reign by force. In the meantime they repudiated allegiance to any other government.

Then in June of the same year there is a splendid entry relating to Francis Foster, a young man from Nottingham, who had travelled to London to gain further experience of the craft of gloving. He took the precaution of getting the Mayor of Nottingham to give him a certificate that he had completed a proper apprenticeship. On arrival in London he needed to become a freeman of the Company of Glovers before he could obtain employment. The certificate reads:

These are to certify to all whom it may concern that Francis Foster of the Town and County of Nottingham Glover, the late apprentice of Joseph Wilkinson of the same Town and County Glover, hath served the said Joseph Wilkinson as a lawful apprentice by the space of seaven years in the trade and occupation of a glover which he now useth in the Town of Nottingham And he the said Francis Foster being desirous to travel in the several parts of this Kingdom of England to work journeyworke for some time the better to increase his experience in the said trade and occupation of a Glover And for his free and safe passing hath prayed the certificate of us the Mayor and Burgesses of the said Town and County of Nottingham Theis are therefore to will and require all his Maties Loveing subjects to permit and suffer the said Francis Foster peaceably and quietly to travel into the City of London or any part thereof within the Kingdom of England as he shall think most convenient for him for the gaining of experience in the trade or occupation of a Glover he the said Francis Foster bearing and behaving himself as becomes an honest man.

In Witness whereof I John Parker Mayor of the said Town have hereunto put my hand and the seal of my Mayoralty the 1st June 1675.

Francis Foster was made free of the Company on redemption paying the Company £4 13s. 6d.

In October 1677 the Company received from the executor of a deceased glover the sum of £5 to benefit the poor of the Company. Immediately afterwards there is an entry where Thomas Bournett 'haveing been an Antient Journeyman' asked the Court if he could not be admitted a master. There was some debate but it is pleasant to record that the Court agreed and he was required to pay £1 7s. 0d. which was substantially less than the proper fee.

Finally, there is an entry relating to the 'Rowling Stone'.[9] A Mrs. Chapman appeared and told the Court that her late husband had sold the Rowling Stone belonging to the Company for 20 shillings which she paid and in consideration of which the Company declared itself satisfied.

During these years the livery seems to have achieved a reasonable degree of numerical strength. Documents in the Corporation of London Record Office show that by 1682,[10] Mr. Richard Gibson being Master and Mr. William Hetherington Clerk, the livery numbered seventy-five. Six years later, in 1688,[11] Mr. Edmond Farding being Master the livery numbered sixty-two.

---

[9] Mr. Roy Thomson, BSc, C.Chem, FRSC, FSLTC, Chief Executive of the Leather Conservation Centre, Northampton, surmises that 'the Rowling Stone' was the stone from an edge runner mill. It could have been used to crush alum or tanning or dyeing materials before they were used by the glover to prepare the skins.

[10] CLRO Companies 3.5.

[11] ibid.

XI

The Company Loses Contact
with the Glove Trade

THERE IS A GAP of almost 100 years from the date when the earliest surviving Minute Book ends in 1679 and the date when the next extant Minute Book begins in 1773. From 1773 to 1804 the minutes of the Court of Assistants are complete. They reflect the routine affairs of a company evidently very different from the Company of the previous century.

The most striking difference is that there is, throughout those 30 years, no reference to the gloving industry. The problems of the search and sealing of leather which had so exercised the minds of previous generations no longer troubled the members of the Company. Indeed, out of a livery which never seems to have fallen below the limit mentioned in the ordinances of 1681 only three or four of the members are described as glovers by trade and only one, Josiah Monnery, Master in 1777, appears to have held office as Master. The rulers of the Company were oilmen and drapers, orange merchants and victuallers. The connection of the Company with the craft of gloving appears to have become tenuous.

The change is also reflected in the business activities of the Company. Whereas the previous century had been characterised by controversy and enthusiasm in tackling the Company's perceived adversaries, whether within the Leathersellers' Company or elsewhere, and whereas that enthusiasm had, on occasion, boiled over into disputes between the Court and the livery and within the Court itself, now all was calm.

The 17th century had called for resolution and a determination to succeed sustained over a long period of time as first the Charter and then acceptance of the Company by the City and the approval of bye-laws and grant of a livery were obtained. As each citadel was stormed another hove into view. Even after the turn of the century the struggle continued, this time to obtain control over working glovers free of other companies. However, in the Minute Books of the last quarter of the 18th century there are no notices of translations either to or from the Company. It is as if, having achieved all its objectives, the Company had, as yet, failed to establish a new purpose and identity and its diverse membership was held together by the looser bonds of habit and tradition. Nevertheless, membership of a company enabled the freedom of the City to be enjoyed[1] and the rights

---

[1] This gave the exclusive right to trade by wholesale and retail within the City, immunity from toll of markets and fairs throughout England, freedom from impressment into the armed forces and the right to elect the City's Aldermen and Common Councillors. It was not until 1835 that it became possible to obtain the freedom of the City without at the same time being free of a company. Jones, *The Corporation of London*, p.220.

attached to membership of the livery[2] were sufficiently important to ensure that there was no shortage of new members coming forward. Looked at dispassionately, the Company of Glovers in 1780 seems nearer to the Company of 1980 than to the Company of 1680.

What then do the minutes reveal of the Company's affairs? At the outset it should be noted that the Court of Assistants met at the *George and Vulture Tavern*, Cornhill, and this was the venue of the Courts throughout the period of which we have knowledge. Evidently the Company's Hall near Beech Lane had been disposed of. This is not really surprising because the Company was not well off. In 1774 the balance of cash due to the Company was £226 3s. 0½d. Over the years it steadily decreased and this shortage of funds greatly restricted the activities open to the livery. The only sources of revenue apart from quarterage were the fees payable on admission to the freedom or to the livery and the fines levied on unwilling stewards or the sums payable on advancement to the Court of Assistants or on election to the office of Warden or Master. Out of these all expenses, including the salaries of the clerk and the beadle, had to be paid. Nevertheless, the Company did not fail in its duty of charity to its poorer members and there are several examples of small sums being paid as, for example, in 1775, 10s. 6d. was given to the widow of a glover 'for her present relief'.[3] In 1781, there is a list of 13 widows to whom pensions were paid, and in 1790 the Court ordered the Clerk to pay to Samuel Brown the sum of one guinea he being in very distressed circumstances 'and an Old Member of this Company', and the following year the same amount was given to Mary Moore for her personal relief. A rather larger sum of five guineas was paid in 1798 to Mr. Thomas Tuke, a poor liveryman, as a 'Charitable Donation'.

When the minutes open in 1774 there is an interesting entry relating to a disputed Parliamentary election for the City constituency. A disappointed candidate, Mr. John Roberts, was alleging malpractice against the successful member, the Right Honourable Frederick Bull, the Lord Mayor. He appealed to the House of Commons for relief. Sir Fletcher Norton, the Speaker, wrote to the Company directing it to produce all its public books, papers and bye-laws to Mr. Roberts or his agents so that they could inspect them and take copies. What Mr. Roberts was alleging was that the Sheriffs, as Returning Officers, allowed several persons to vote for the Lord Mayor who, he believed, had no right to vote, 'and by several illegal and improper practices and other undue means and proceedings' a pretended majority was obtained by the Lord Mayor. Mr. Roberts believed he had a clear majority of valid votes.

The Court of Assistants was reluctant to produce the Company's books and papers to be examined by a stranger and the Clerk was instructed to prepare a case for the opinion of the Recorder as to the legality of the Speaker's order.

[2]   From 1475 the right to vote in Common Hall and elect the Lord Mayor, sheriffs and some other City officers and, until 1832, the exclusive right to elect the City's members of parliament. The privilege of voting in Common Hall was confirmed by statute in 1725 (11 Geo. I c 18) which required that electors should be freemen of the City and liverymen of at least one year's standing. Jones, *The Corporation of London*, p.10. The same statute confirmed the exclusive right of liverymen to elect the members of Parliament for the City, a privilege they had enjoyed from the 16th century. The Reform Act of 1832 gave the vote to inhabitant householders and occupiers of the annual value of £10 but preserved the rights of the liverymen provided their freedom was acquired by servitude or patrimony derived from a father free by servitude, and the liveryman resided within seven miles of the City. Jones, *The Corporation of London*, p.15.
[3]   See Guildhall Library MS 4591 for this and subsequent references taken from the Minute books.

The Recorder's opinion is quoted in the minutes. It is quite short and worth repeating:

> I think the order to [*sic*] loose and general and in many parts exceptionable. I am disabled by my seat in the House to give an opinion as a lawyer upon the subject but am inclined to advise the Company to comply with the order if the search is conducted with decency and by a small number only. The Officers of the Company may specify to Mr. Roberts' Agents that they do this act out of an inclination to produce everything that may thro' light upon the Question not thinking themselves under any legal obligation from the order.

The Court of Assistants accepted that advice but directed their Clerk or his clerk to be present when any papers were examined.

It was at the next Quarterly Court that the Court of Assistants decided to enlarge the livery. They seem to have devoted time to carrying out research into the historical background but there is no indication that they ever approached the City authorities. They argued that they believed they were free to amend the bye-laws of the Company without restraint, that there had been a considerable increase in the number of freemen and some had been made liverymen despite the fact that the number thereby exceeded one hundred and twenty. Many more freemen would like to join the livery but feared to do so on the 'ill grounded fear that their Franchises or right of voting at Elections would, upon a Scrutiny, be invalidated by such Bye-laws'.

The Court, having regard to the constitution of the City, and particularly an ordinance of Common Hall of the 49th of Edward III and two Acts of Common Council of the 7th and 15th of Edward IV, whereby Common Hall ought to be representative of all the companies, believed they were free to amend their bye-laws 'as occasion may require provided they are not repugnant to the Act of 19 Henry VII or the law of the land or the constitution of the City'. Therefore, to prevent future objections, they repealed that part of the ordinances limiting the number of liverymen.

From that time the Company has considered that it has an unlimited livery and there is no doubt that that resolution has had a profound effect on the development of the Company two centuries later.

It may be useful, at this point, to look at the numbers of apprentices, freemen and liverymen within the Company about this time. Fortunately, there are a few helpful sources of reference. Among the archives of the Company at Guildhall are a Register of Freedom Admissions for the period 1738 to 1851,[4] a Register of Apprentice Bindings from 1694 to 1794,[5] a late 18th-century livery list or quarterage account[6] and a number of miscellaneous papers relating to apprentice bindings, freedom admissions and livery and Court lists between 1776 and 1780.[7]

The Poll of the Liverymen of the City of London, referred to earlier, revealed that by 1710 the livery had increased to 120, the limit prescribed by the Ordinances, of whom 102 had voted at the election in October of that year. By way of comparison the Poll showed that the Fletchers' livery numbered 17 and that of the Musicians twenty-five.

One of the surviving papers, which is an account of quarterage payments listed as a 'livery list arranged by streets' but which may also include freemen, is undated. It is late

---

[4]   Guildhall Library MS 4592.   [5]   Guildhall Library MS 4593.   [6]   Guildhall Library MS 2912.
[7]   Guildhall Library MS 2918.

18th-century and thought to relate to the year 1778. This 'livery' list contains 300 names. There is also a list of the Worshipful Company of Glovers for the year 1779 (five years after the resolution to abolish any limit on the livery). The list contains 326 names though 35 are marked as 'dead' and four are marked 'gone away', 'gone into country', 'gone abroad' and 'at Boston in America'. So there was apparently the very substantial and, perhaps, surprising number of 287 members, though it remains unclear how many were of the livery.

Moreover, numbers of young men and a few young women continued to enter into apprenticeships. In the Glovers' archive there is a Register of Apprentice Bindings for the period from 1735 to 1748.[8] In 13½ years a total of 341 apprentices, including 10 girls, were bound.[9] A mere 32 of those apprentices were sons of freemen or liverymen of the Company. The list includes two apprentices who afterwards became Masters of the Company, Josiah Monnery, Master in 1776/7 who was by trade a glover, and James Peircy from Easingwold in the North Riding of Yorkshire, a sugar baker, Master in 1773/4 and Master when the Company resolved that its livery should be unlimited. The Register shows the name of the apprentice, the name and occupation of his or her father, the name of the master to whom bound and the date of the apprenticeship. In addition, there is a later volume; that covering the apprentice bindings for 100 years from 1694 to 1794.[10] The volume bears the subsidiary title of 'The Orphan's Register'.[11] Under a 1694 statute 'for the relief of orphans and other creditors of the City of London' it was required that apprentices should pay on their binding a tax or duty. The arrangement continued until 1861. The new apprentice paid 2s. 6d. to the Company concerned and, from time to time, the Company accounted to the City's Chamberlain. So there was a fiscal as well as an administrative need to keep records of apprenticeships. Moreover, as long ago as 1294 it was ordered 'that the better and more discreet engaged in their several trades of the City shall cause a register to be made of all the names of masters, their apprentices and servants',[12] and by statute[13] the Companies had to 'keep in their Common Halls one or more book or books of vellum or parchment in which every such sum shall be set down and the name of the apprentice who paid the same'.

The 'orphans' debt' was extinguished in 1820 but the Chamberlain collected the tax until 1861.[14]

In the first six months of the Register of Apprentices 24 new apprenticeships were registered and they continued steadily throughout the period recorded. The register ends in January 1797. By then payment from the Company to the Chamberlain was being made at increasingly lengthy intervals. In July 1774, £42 2s. 6d. was paid in respect of 337 apprenticeships and the last payment in January 1797 is of £48 17s. 6d. for 391 apprenticeships.

Some unusual names occur. Examples are Melchior Gamon, Parthenia Watson, Caleb Kettlebutter, Dulcibeler Todd, Baptist Larkins, Turnpenny Syrett, Bathya Chambers,

8   Guildhall Library MS 4593.
9   Girls could be bound apprentice and a woman could be a member of a company while she was a spinster or a widow. E. Austin, *The Law relating to Apprentices, including those bound according to the Custom of the City of London* (London, 1890), p.118.
10   Guildhall Library MS 4593.
11   The Chamberlain was the Accountant General of the Court of Orphans under the ancient City custom whereby the Mayor and Aldermen were by law the trustees of the orphans of the citizens. Jones, *The Corporation of London*, p.110.
12   Sharpe, *Calendar of Letter Books*, Letter Book B, p.241.   13   5 & 6 William & Mary c 10.
14   See C.R.H. Cooper, *The Archives of the City of London Livery Companies and Related Organisations* (Guildhall Library, 1985), p.21.

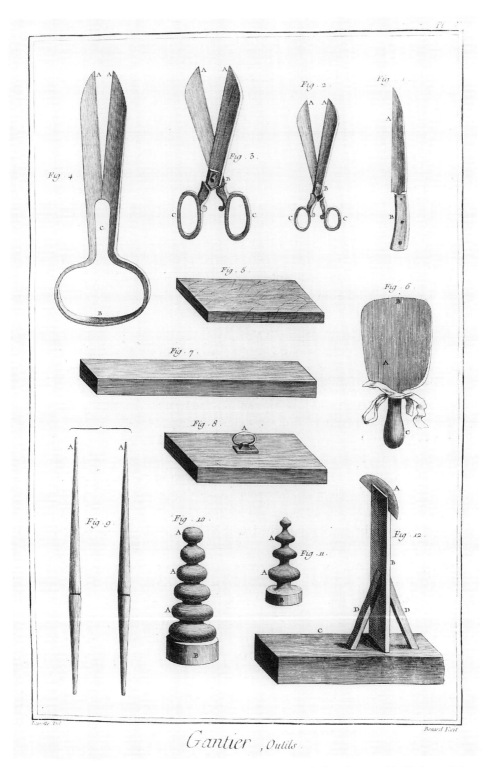

Gantier, Outils.

12   *Diderot's Encyclopédie*, Tome IV, 1764. Glove-making tools including shears and knife (items 1-4), a doling slab and knife (5 and 6), weights (7 and 8), gauges and measures (9-11), and a staking beam (12).

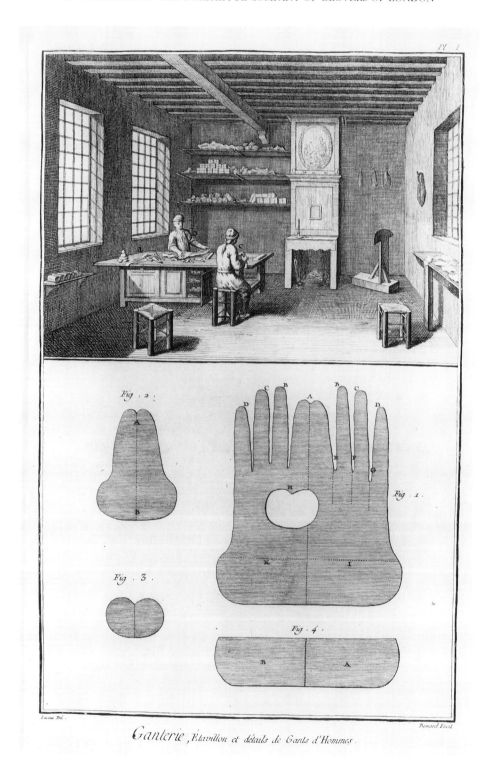

13   *Diderot's Encyclopédie*, Tome IV, 1764. A glover's workshop. The man in the background is examining a skin before it is cut and his companion is stitching a glove. Underneath are shown sections of men's gloves before being stitched together.

Pasquan Baillon, Habakhuk Pride, and Puryour Box. Throughout, there continued to occur the occasional apprenticeship of girls.

It was also necessary to keep a record of freemen admitted to the Company and the date of their freedom. Fortunately, three books or registers of freedom admissions have survived.[15] They cover quite an extensive period. The first is from 1738 to 1748, the second book records freedoms between 1748 and 1785 and the last book carries the register forward to 1851. It will be convenient to examine them all together.

From time to time the registers are marked as 'examined' and there follows a signature. This was for the purpose of checking that stamp duty had been paid. An Act of 1694[16] required that a duty of 1s. was payable on every admission into any corporation or company. The duty payable was increased over the years and indeed it continued to be payable until 1949 when the Act was repealed, at which time the stamp duty stood at £1 payable on taking up freedom by patrimony or servitude and £3 for those acquiring freedom by redemption.

Initially, the registers each contain three columns showing the date of admission, then the name of the freeman and finally the method by which admission is gained. If admission is by servitude or patrimony the register also shows the name of the master or the father of the applicant as the case may be.

The first register covering a period of eight and a half years shows that 306 applicants were admitted by redemption, 71 by servitude and a mere 14 by patrimony. Nineteen were women. The rate of admission was high: over three a month. A different pattern has emerged from that revealed by the 17th-century Minute Book. There, the majority of freemen were arriving by way of servitude and admission by redemption was much rarer. Here the positions have been reversed.

The second register does not include quite as much detail as the first. After July 1759 there are only two columns giving a date and the name of the new freeman. This is the pattern followed in the third register. From 1749 until 1759 there were 221 admissions of which 90 were by redemption, 114 by servitude and, again, a small number, 17, by patrimony. Seven women were included. From July 1759 to June 1785 the information to break down the admissions into categories is not available. No less than 667 men and 14 women were admitted, an average of between two and three a month. During the years covered by the third register a total of 577 men and six women were admitted. Four years are omitted from the record altogether. There are no entries for the years 1794-7. Over the whole period the average has fallen to over one admission to the freedom each month. There is no specific point at which the numbers begin to drop off; the evidence is more of a steady decline. In the 19th century the number of freemen admitted each year rarely ran into double figures and never at all after 1834. Between 1846 and 1851 inclusive only 13 members were admitted to the freedom.

While there is a good deal of information about the numbers of freemen there is little hard evidence about the strength of the livery. However, the policy of the Company seems to have been to encourage freemen to take up the livery as and when they were

---

[15] Guildhall Library MS 4592.   [16] 5 & 6 William & Mary c 21.

able to do so. Doubtless a factor borne in mind was the financial benefit resulting to the Company.

Quarterage remained difficult to collect. The late 18th-century quarterage list among the Company's papers shows many arrears and many familiar excuses. The words 'gone away', 'will not pay' and 'can't afford to pay' occur. There are only two practising glovers: Thomas Turner of Fleet Street and William Flack of Strand.

Amongst the miscellaneous papers now surviving are several lists of those in nomination for membership of the Court of Assistants[17] and it is possible to see the varying period of time which elapsed between a member becoming free and afterwards attaining the livery. Benjamin Robertson who was employed in the Navy Office (Master in 1783) took the livery immediately on being made free in 1758 as did Robert Lewin who was secretary to the Board of Directors of the Bank of England and was Master in 1779 and some others. For many the period between admission to the freedom and the livery was up to 10 years or more. Richard Draper, who became Master in 1781 took up the livery 19 years after becoming a freeman.

It is possible also in certain instances to calculate the interval between a member taking the livery and becoming Master of the Company. At each stage of advancement the procedure was democratic. Lists were prepared of those senior and eligible for admission to the Court of Assistants. Up to a score of members would be nominated and voted upon by the Court. Then the positions of First and Second Warden and Renter Warden and, eventually, the office of Master were similarly put to the vote with the names of two or three candidates put forward on each occasion.

John William Anderson who afterwards became Master was obviously an exceptional candidate. He was admitted to the livery in 1789 and made Master in 1794/5. William Griffiths and John Pollard, Masters in 1782 and 1774 respectively, each waited nine years for that office. For some the period was much longer. Among those cases examined, William Platell, Master in 1793, reached that office after an interval of 35 years. In the case of Richard Ladyman, Master in 1792, the interval was 40 years and in the case of William Eamonson, Master in 1797, the interval was 42 years, though in these three instances the period is calculated from the date of admission to the freedom.

Amongst those who were Master in the 1770s and 1780s, William Parry was a linen draper, William Eamonson an oylman, John Pollard a tobacconist, James Piercy a sugar baker, John Kentish a jeweller and William Wryghte a wine merchant. They reflect the diversity of occupations of the membership. It would be tedious to list all the trades involved but in addition to the more usual ones were those of bricklayer, breeches maker, lottery office keeper, bookseller, pawnbroker, indigo maker, seedsman, cheesemonger, china burner, blueman, attorney, silversmith, cabinet maker, Manchester man and even leatherseller.

It is, perhaps, surprising that throughout the latter part of the 18th century the Company was able to maintain its numerical strength. It is clear that the trade of gloving had declined dramatically and the connection with the craft was negligible. Moreover, the Company was so poor it had little to offer members. Dr. I.G. Doolittle[18] suggests that

---

[17]   Guildhall Library MS 2917.
[18]   I.G. Doolittle, *The City of London and its Livery Companies* (Dorchester, 1982), p.15. (Hereafter Doolittle, *The City of London.*)

some of the smaller Companies went to great lengths to induce new members to join them. As he put it,

> the smaller Companies … could look forward to no resolution of their (financial) difficulties from their property returns, which were too meagre to offer lasting relief. Instead, they turned to their members for help. The fines of those Companies were low enough to attract those who were interested only in securing a vote in Guildhall elections or participating in City life. An influx of freemen redemptioners or a call on the livery could be invaluable in the fight against insolvency. How valuable may be judged from the assiduous assistance given to those market forces. The Chamberlain's officials were encouraged by gratuities to direct newly admitted freemen towards certain enterprising Companies. Other Companies offered similar incentives to their own officers.

There is a suggestion that gratuities of that kind may have been paid by the Glovers' Company. Among the Company's records are the following notes:[19]

Edward Barlington of the Parish of St. James Clerkenwell Middlesex Victualler made free of
Glovers   £1. 12.   6.
                                                                         livery   6.
                                                                                              7. 12.   6.
                                         Gave the man who bro^{t} him   1.   1.   0.
                                                                                          £6. 11.   6.

12th August 1778
William Pickard of Botolph Lane London Orange Merchant made free of Glovers
                                                        brought by Greig £1. 12.   6.
                                                               gave Greig   1.   1.   0.
                                                                                        11.   6.

3rd Sept^{r}
Robert Simpson of Fleet Street London the corner of Fetter Lane oilman made free of
Glovers   bro't by Greig £1. 12.   6.
                                                                 gave Phil.   10.
                                                                                    1.   2.   0.

and there are other entries, several involving Mr. Greig who seems to have been busy on behalf of the Company. Despite such efforts, however, the Company remained in straightened circumstances throughout this period.

---

[19] Guildhall Library MS 2917. These are notes written on slips of paper apparently as temporary memoranda which have survived.

XII

Problems of Finance Occur

THE ABSENCE OF CONCERN for the craft of gloving caused by the decline of the trade in London did not mean that the Court of Assistants were lacking in matters of business.

In 1774 the Company made arrangements for a dinner for the livery on Lord Mayor's Day.[1] There was the usual difficulty in securing the services of four Stewards. The actual arrangements are set out in the minutes.

> Ordered that Mr. Davies provide the usual quantity of strong and small beer.

> Ordered that Mr. Molliner [*sic*] the cook provide the Dinner … and that he be allowed for the same £ [amount left blank].

> Ordered that Mr. Whittaker provide the following Musick … vizt. two French Horns, one Bassoon and three Heautboys[2] and that he be allowed for the same £ [amount left blank].

> Ordered that the usual number of tickets be prepared and sealed.

> Ordered that Mr. Maskall provide the following quantity of wine: Sixteen dozen of Red Port,[3] six dozen of Lisbon, one dozen of Mountain[4] and one dozen of Rhenish.

The same dinner was approved the following year the only difference being that on that occasion the minutes show that Mr. Molineux, the cook, was to be allowed £38. The livery was treated to dinner the following year too and on this occasion Mr. Molineux's allowance had risen to £42 but the first signs of change were appearing. It was resolved that the livery 'do not walk out or use the Stand on that day'.

In January 1778 there is another reference to the Company's bye-laws of 1681. These required the four Wardens at their own expense four times a year, that is on every Quarter Court Day, to provide dinner for the Court of Assistants with a fine in default. However, it was now considered that 'the penalty or forfeiture of forty shillings … however fully sufficient and effectual it might have been in the year 1680 to answer the purposes thereby intended, has, from the great distance of time and the many alterations of circumstances … been by experience at length found unproportioned and inadequate'. The Court therefore increased the fine to £10.

By 1783 the balance of the Company's cash in the Renter Warden's hands was only £105 12s. 0d.[5] In the following year the Court of Assistants, concerned at the poor

---

[1] Guildhall Library MS 4591. [2] A wooden double-reed instrument of high pitch forming a treble to the bassoon.
[3] As opposed to white port. The old name for port. [4] A variety of Malaga wine.
[5] Guildhall Library MS 4591.

attendance of its members, ordered that the fine for non-attendance, fixed at 5s. in 1681, be increased to 10s. 6d. Two members of the Court who had been elected 'long since' had neither attended nor paid the admission fine of £3. They were to be warned that an action would be commenced against them. Then, in October 1784, there is the rather sad entry that the Company's 'Stand with its Appendages', brought out for the livery's use on Lord Mayor's Day, should be disposed of for the benefit of the Company.

In 1784, also, the Clerk, Mr. Roberts, died. His death was reported to the Court on 17 December and it was ordered that a new clerk be elected on the 20th, surprisingly only three days later. During those three days Mr. Philip Wyatt Crowther was to do the Company's business. He did not neglect the opportunity to petition for the office himself and in due course he was elected. His first task was to look through the Company's books to discover which liverymen 'appeared to be the most ancient and fit to be put in nomination' to fill up the vacancy in the Assistants to the Company.

Faced with the continuing problem of getting freemen to serve as Stewards, the Court, in 1785, resolved to keep a book listing the freemen by seniority specifying the dates of admission and the offices they had served or fined for. There were other problems concerning the dinner but of a different kind. It was

> likewise the Opinion of this committee that the great Confusion and Indecorum that has hitherto prevailed in the Upper Room at Bakers Hall on Lord Mayor's Day can only be prevented by the Wardens for the time being presiding at the Head of each Table which the committee recommend to be done in future.

To the obvious surprise of the Court in 1787 they found a willing Steward. William Hooper appeared and asked to be allowed to serve in that office. He was told it would be attended with a very considerable additional expense but he still entreated that he be permitted to serve. He also asked if he could join the livery. Both requests were agreed to.

Although there was a dinner on Lord Mayor's Day 1790 when the livery numbering 180 dined together at the Globe Tavern Fleet Street at a cost of 3s. 6d. per head there was no dinner the following year. The minutes show that the Court concluded that the funds would not permit the Company to provide a dinner for the livery. In fact, except during the Mayoral years of Alderman Burnell and Alderman Anderson, no more livery dinners appear to have been held on Lord Mayor's Day during the period to 1804 when the minutes end.

Instead, in October 1792,[6] in order to establish a fund to prevent the necessity of calling upon the freemen 'who are not in circumstances to pay', the Court resolved that its members would dine together on Election Day only and that the sum of £20 should be paid by the person entitled to provide the customary dinner in lieu thereof, and that all such sums should be invested in the names of the three senior members of the Court in the purchase of 3% Consolidated Bank Annuities. The following February Mr. Platell, a member of the Court, paid £20 in lieu of providing a dinner. Then, in October, the Court rescinded the previous year's resolution. Belatedly, it was appreciated that such dinners were not paid for out of the funds of the Company but at the expense of the

---

6 ibid.

individual members of the Court. Whether it was a coincidence or not there was a nil attendance at the Quarterly Courts in the following January, April and July, and in October 1795 it was resolved that the Court would dine together on the customary days but when there was no Warden present in rotation to provide the dinner the members of the Court would share the expense, each subscribing one guinea.

In November 1797 the livery fine was increased from £5 13s. 4d. to £10 in a fresh attempt to improve the Company's finances. It failed to do so. Sadly, in June 1800, a committee examining the Company's accounts reported a deficit, 'payments exceeded the receipts by the sum of £3 6s. 5d.' Moreover, there was due to Mr. Holdsworth 'for entertaining the Company on the Election Days (there being no Master to defray the expense) the sum of £71 6s. 7d.' The committee considered 'the most eligible mode' for discharging the debt 'and it appearing by the Custom of the Company that every Gentleman serving the Offices of Master and Wardens are to provide five Dinners'; they found that

> Messrs. Fisher, Parker, Ladyman, Anderson and Rowlatt by reason of Vacancies in the said Offices, had only provided four Dinners each. And the committee having inspected the Order of this Court of the 25th October 1792 which directed that Twenty pounds should be paid in lieu of providing the customary Dinner do unanimously resolve to recommend it to the Court to request each of those Gentlemen to pay that sum in lieu of the Dinner which they have not been called upon to provide in consequence of the vacancies in the said offices; which will enable your committee not only to discharge the several Bills now remaining due, but those which will be necessarily incurred upon the Election Days until by the regular rotation being restored the necessity will cease to exist.

The Court was pleased to approve the committee's recommendation.

Money problems continued to dog the Company during these years. On 28 October 1802 it was ordered that 'it be referred to the Court of Assistants of this Company to consider the State of the Company's Finances and report'. What they reported does not appear in the Company's minutes. In April 1803, Mr. Crowther, the Clerk, died. His successor, Mr. John Thomas, took over the balance of the Company's funds in his hands amounting to £39 18s. 0d. However, when the Renter Warden's accounts were audited it was found that the Company 'were considerably indebted' to the estate of Mr. Crowther. Sir John Anderson volunteered the sum of £10 10s. 0d. towards discharge of this debt. It seems clear that the Company's finances were not well run. After Mr. Crowther's death it was discovered that Sir John Anderson who had already served as Lord Mayor and Sir Richard Welch who had served as Sheriff had not taken up their livery or paid their livery fines.

Throughout the years covered by these Minute Books from 1773 to 1804 there are one or two matters reported which throw light on the wider concerns of the period. For example, in 1780, William Rix, the Town Clerk, wrote asking for the Company's aid in paying the expense of maintaining the troops sent into the City for the protection of property 'during the late Riotts'. This is clearly a reference to the Gordon Riots which created great damage and loss of life in London that year. They developed from a protest against the passing of the Catholic Relief Act turning into mob violence. No doubt the

Company was not in a position to offer much aid. It was ordered that the letter lie on the table.

A more mundane request was received in November 1785. The Stamp Office wrote complaining about persons selling gloves 'without having the proper Stamps affixed previous to the Sale thereof'. The Commissioners of Stamp Duties considered that a public notice from the Company would be helpful both to them and to the tradesmen. They were sure that the Company would help. If those in London, Westminster and Southwark could be induced to stamp their goods for sale they believed the example would be followed by country dealers. A week later the Clerk replied. A special court had been convened and the Company's charter and bye-laws had been examined but the Court found that their powers were confined to the survey and correction of frauds and abuses in making gloves and the deceitful tanning of leather. They therefore had no power to regulate the inconveniences complained of.

In June 1789, rather curiously, five Liverpool merchants were made free of the Company by redemption. Again, in March 1793 two merchants from Kirkham in Lancashire and one from Liverpool were made free by redemption. The same thing happened again in 1796 and 1797 when four more Liverpool merchants and one from Warrington were made free. No doubt they wished to acquire the right to trade in the City.

A happy entry occurs in 1799. On 25 April it was resolved unanimously by the Court 'that the Freedom of this Company be presented to Captain Sir Edward Berry for his eminent services rendered his King and Country in the Battle of the Nile on the 1st day of August 1798'. Mr. Crowther was ordered to attend Sir Edward bearing that resolution. At the Quarterly Court in July Mr. Crowther produced Sir Edward's reply in the following terms:

> Kensington 2nd May 1799
>
> Sir
> I was yesterday favor'd with your Letter inclosing the unanimous Resolution of the Glovers Company and beg you will present to them my best thanks for the honor they have been pleased to confer on me – at the same time I request you will assure the Company – that under the Flag of Rear Admiral Lord Nelson, I claim <u>no</u> other Merit, than <u>obeying</u> his Lordship's Commands
> I am
> Sir
> You very humble Serv't
>
> E. Berry

He was made free on 8 August.

In 1802, Richard Welch, a member of the Company, was elected Sheriff. Sixteen members of the Court were instructed to attend him on the solemnities of taking office 'as has been usual and customary upon the like occasions'. Moreover, it was ordered that the Sheriffs elect have the use of the Company's colours but that no new colour be provided.

XIII

A Trio of Lord Mayors

IN THE 18TH CENTURY the Glovers' Company produced three Lord Mayors. The first, and perhaps the most celebrated of the three, Alderman Sir John Barnard, was mentioned in Chapter IX when he was translated to the Grocers' Company in 1737 immediately prior to becoming Lord Mayor. He was also one of the City's Members of Parliament. He is described by Valerie Hope in her book *My Lord Mayor*[1] as

> the outstanding Lord Mayor in the first half of the eighteenth century and (he) led the popular forces in the City for over twenty years. He was born in Reading, the son of Quaker parents, but joined the Church of England before he was twenty. He began work at fifteen in his father's counting house, then came to London, joined the Glovers' Company, translating to the Grocers' Company when he became Lord Mayor. He had great financial ability and made marine insurance his main business. In 1737 Walpole was said to have offered him the Chancellorship of the Exchequer but Sir John absolutely refused it, saying it was a laborious and envied place 'by which he could honestly get but £4000 a year, and so much he gets by his trade without trouble.' He and Walpole clashed later that year when Walpole turned down his scheme for reducing interest on the National Debt from 4% to 3%.

She adds that he rallied popular support during the Jacobite Rebellion of 1745 and in 1747 his statue by Scheemakers was erected in the Royal Exchange.[2] He had, she says,

> worked hard to ameliorate the condition of poor debtors, to raise the standard of London policing and to suppress begging … After his Mayoralty he wrote a little booklet for his apprentices. It was called 'a present for an Apprentice; a sure guide to gain both esteem and an estate.' It is given to all freemen of the City of London as Rules for the Conduct of life … He died in 1764 aged nearly eighty and was buried in Mortlake church.

Sadly, no memorial to him survives and his very grave is said to have been covered up by an extension to the church.[3]

Because the Company's records for the first half of the 18th century are missing we have no information about his life in the Company or the offices he held.

We do, however, have information about the Company's next Lord Mayor, Alderman John Burnell, who represented Aldgate Ward. Valerie Hope says of him that he was a

---

[1] Valerie Hope, *My Lord Mayor* (London, 1989), p.110 *et seq.* (Hereafter Hope, *My Lord Mayor*.)
[2] It is not there now and seems to have disappeared long ago. It was made of marble and at the time it was raised was remarkable in that the only other non-royal statue in the Exchange was of Gresham. See Ann Saunders (ed.), *The Royal Exchange* (London, 1997). When he retired in 1747, Sir John was thanked in the Guildhall 'for the honour and influence which the City had on many occasions derived from the dignity of his conduct, for his firm adhesion to the constitution, both in Church and State; his noble struggles for liberty and disinterested and valuable pursuit of the glory and prosperity of his king and country uninfluenced by power, unawed by clamour and unbiased by the prejudice of party'. J. Aubrey Rees, *The English Tradition* (London, 1934), p.205. Such words have proved a more enduring memorial than the Scheemakers statue.
[3] Information given to First Under Warden Alan Howarth by the Church archivist.

target for John Wilkes' wit. He 'became Lord Mayor in 1787 aged 84, the oldest Lord Mayor ever. He began life as a working stonemason. At a City banquet he was very awkward about cutting open a pie. 'You had better take a trowel to it,' shouted Wilkes.[4]

In the Company's livery list of 1779 John Burnell is shown as a bricklayer and his address is given as Green Street, Leicester Fields. In 1778 he was Renter Warden and the Minute Book[5] records that he was a Sheriff elect for the City of London and County of Middlesex for the year ensuing. He requested that 16 members of the Court of Assistants 'attend him on the Solemnities of the 28th and 30th of this month (September) as has been usual and customary upon the like occasions'. That was agreed to and it was resolved that the Company would pay and bear 'a proper

14   Sir John Barnard, Lord Mayor 1737.

proportion or half part of the charges of providing a Barge for the 30th instant and other incidental Expenses usually paid by the Companies of which the Sheriffs are members'. It was ordered that the Sheriffs elect might, if they wished, have the use of the Company's colours on that day.

Moving forward to 1787,[6] it is interesting to see the procedures involved when Alderman Burnell became Lord Mayor. However, all did not go smoothly between him and the Company and it seems a shame that the parties did not cooperate harmoniously. The Company's minutes tell the story. On 4 October 1787 it was resolved 'that a committee consisting of the Master, Wardens, Father and the three senior members of the Court, do wait on Mr. Alderman Burnell the Lord Mayor elect respecting the necessary regulations for next Lord Mayor's Day'.

On 16 October there was a special Court attended by Alderman Burnell and two Wardens and two Assistants.

> The Delegation having represented to the Lord Mayor Elect that the ensuing Lord Mayor's Day would necessarily be attended by an Expense which the Finances of the Company were not able to sustain his Lordship was requested to pay the extra Expense that will be incurred by reason of their attending his Lordship upon that Occasion.

The Lord Mayor elect having offered the sum of £20 it 'is ordered that an Estimation of such additional Expense be laid before the Committee at their next Court and they do adjourn ye consideration thereof till that Court.'

---

[4]   Hope, *My Lord Mayor*, p.150.   [5]   Guildhall Library MS 4591.   [6]   ibid.

On 25 October the committee gave their report which said,

We of your Committee to whom it was on the 8th day of September last referred to settle the Stewards and other Matters for the ensuing Lord Mayor's Day do certify that on the 8th instant we appointed a Delegation consisting of the Master Wardens and three of the senior Members of the said Committee to attend the Right Honourable the Lord Mayor Elect and to represent to his Lordship that the Finances of the Company were not adequate to sustain the additional Expense that would necessarily be incurred in attending his Lordship in the customary procession on that Day and to request that his Lordship would on that Account be pleased to defray such extra Expense.

The Delegation reported to your Committee that on the 16th instant they held a Conference with his Lordship upon this subject who declined paying the whole of such Expence but offered the sum of twenty pounds in aid thereof; they thereupon directed an estimate of such additional Expense to be prepared and laid before your Committee at their next Meeting which was accordingly done and is hereunto annexed.

Your Committee beg leave further to observe that on the 18th instant we took the said Estimate into our consideration and having investigated the State of the Company's Accounts and examined the List of the several Freemen We were unanimously of Opinion that it would be an act of Injustice to the said Freemen to attempt to compel them to pay the said Expence which in the Judgment of your Committee (grounded upon such Examination) cou'd not be raised without being attended with great personal Inconvenience. We therefore feel it is our indispensible Duty to represent these several Facts to this Court and to recommend that the Livery do not walk upon the ensuing Lord Mayor's Day unless his Lordship will be pleased to defray such extra Expence in which case your Committee will with the greatest cheerfulness take upon themselves the additional Burthen of regulating the said procession and at the same time pay the strictest attention to all possible economy.

Your Committee lament the inability of the Company (without his Lordship's acquiescence in their request) to pay him those Honors which their Inclinations prompt them to do; they therefore recommend the following Resolutions for the Adoption of this Court as a Tribute of their Esteem and respect

Resolved Unanimously

That this Court will pay his Lordship every personal respect and attention in their power and for that purpose Sixteen of the Assistants will attend his Lordship on Wednesday the 8th of November next upon his Lordship's Inauguration at Guildhall.

Resolved Unanimously

That his Lordship have if he shall desire the same the use of this Company's Colours on that and the following Day.

All which we submit to the Judgment of this Court.

That report is signed by five members of the committee including three former Masters. The estimate of extra expenses for attending the Lord Mayor is attached:

	£	s.	d.			
Mr. Sibley for Ribbands as under						
24 Favors for Company)						
40 Favors for the Marshal's Horses)	5.	6.	8.			
11 Broad Silk Sashes	9.	12.	6.			
2 City Marshal's Scarfs	3.	3.	0.	18.	2.	2.
Painter						
Lord Mayor's Banner	14.					
Company's Banner	9.					
Poles for Colours	5.			28.		
Music				8.	18.	6.
10 Men to bear the Colours				2.	10.	0.
6 Whifflers[7]				1.	10.	0.
2 Constables					10.	0.
4 Boys				1.	0.	0.
Caps Jackets etc. for the Standard Bearers abt.				2.		
				62.	10.	8.

Besides the Expence of the Livery waiting in the Neighbourhood of Blackfriars[8] till his Lordship's return from Westminster.

That report was approved by the Court and a copy was ordered to be sent to Alderman Burnell with the names of 16 members of the Court who would attend him on 8 November.

> Ordered that this Court will go in Coaches on that Day and that the Clerk do communicate the Intention of this Court to the Bowyers[9] Company.
> Ordered that the Clerk do provide a sufficient number of Coaches and the several other matters that may be necessary.

No doubt it could be shown that a great deal of embarrassment might have been avoided if Alderman Burnell had arranged to be translated to one of the Great Twelve companies. This was not always a formality and from 1742 many Lord Mayors elect did not choose to do so. It was held that such translation was not essential.

The saddest aspect of this difference over expense occurred the following November when Alderman Burnell's year of office drew to its end. On 24 October 1788 the Clerk represented to the Company that the Lord Mayor being a freeman of the Company

> it was their indispensible Duty to appoint sixteen of their Members (being Liverymen) to attend his Lordship on Saturday the 8th November next being the Inauguration of the Chief Magistrate and having deliberated upon the said Notification it was resolved unanimously.
> That this Court will at all times discharge in the most respectful manner every official Duty they owe to the Office of Chief Magistrate of this City and that the following Gentlemen being Members of this Court will attend upon that Occasion; but from his

---

[7] A body of attendants armed with a staff and wearing a chain, employed to keep the way clear for a procession at some public spectacle.

[8] The mayoral procession was by barge to Westminster returning to Blackfriars and thence to Guildhall. The livery would require refreshment while waiting the return of the Lord Mayor.

[9] The Company of the outgoing Lord Mayor.

Lordship's unhandsome conduct to the Company they decline dining with him on that Day.

The resolution is signed by the Master, Mr. Hustler, two Wardens and 13 members of the Court of Assistants.

It was further resolved that the above resolutions be signed by the Clerk and delivered to the Right Honourable the Lord Mayor to prevent him sustaining any expense on account of their official attendance and that the Clerk wait upon the Master and Wardens of the Company of Stationers[10] and represent to them the intention of the Court to attend the procession in carriages.

Whether the Lord Mayor's 'unhandsome conduct' was his failure to pay for the special expenses which the Company would have incurred on Lord Mayor's Day or whether there was some other cause of offence it is impossible to say, but the Company's resolution must have been a shock to him. It drew from the Lord Mayor a most dignified and honourable response designed to make his peace with the Company. A special Court was held on 6 November 1788 to consider his letter in reply which reads:

> Mansion House 6th Novr 1788
>
> Gentlemen,
>
> Having received from Mr. Crowther the Resolutions of the Court of Assistants expressive of their Intention not to honor me with their Company to Dinner on the 8th inst. I beg leave to observe that it gives me extreme concern that my Brethren of the Court should feel themselves offended at any part of my Behaviour - for I do most sincerely assure them that I never had the most distant idea of treating with Disrespect Gentlemen for whom as well individually as collectively I have ever entertained the greatest Esteem - And I trust they will therefore be pleased to add to the Felicity and Harmony of that Day, by rescinding their former Resolutions; which will confer the highest Obligation and be ever remembered with the greatest pleasure and satisfaction by
>
> Gentlemen
> Your obedient servant
> John Burnell.
> Mayor.

That letter had no effect on the Court's earlier decision. It was resolved unanimously to transmit the following reply to the Lord Mayor:

> That it was not without the most mature Deliberation and a degree of concern for the Necessity that the Court of Assistants of the Glovers Company adopted the Resolutions of which your Lordship are pleased to express your concern – these Resolutions having been unanimously confirmed by a General Quarterly Court they cannot comply with your Lordship's request to rescind.

The Company had even fined the Lord Mayor (with others) for his non-attendance at Court meetings during his year of office, a policy which seems severe having regard to his Mayoral duties.

---

[10] The Company of the incoming Lord Mayor.

The Lord Mayor did not long survive. He died in 1790, the same year in which Alderman John William Anderson was admitted to the Court of Assistants. John William Anderson lived in Adelphi Terrace. He was elected Alderman in 1789 representing Aldergate Ward. By 1791 Alderman Anderson had become a Warden of the Company and was one of the Sheriffs elect.[11] As was customary, he requested that 16 members of the Court should attend him on his election. The Court agreed and resolved and ordered that the Company would pay half the cost of providing a barge 'and other incidental Expenses usually paid by the Companies of which the Sheriff are members.' It was also resolved that the Sheriffs elect should have, if they wished, the use of the Company's colours.

Only three years later, in 1794, Alderman Anderson was elected Master of the Company and his election as Lord Mayor of London swiftly followed in 1797. In September of that year the Court of Assistants resolved to have a dinner for half the liverymen 'in case the Funds of the Company shall appear to the next Court adequate to the Expense and that Stewards be now appointed but that they do not walk out or use the Stand on that day'.

Following the Lord Mayor's election a special Court was convened to consider 'the necessary Regulations to be adopted on Lord Mayor's Day.' As usual, 16 members were to attend the Lord Mayor on his inauguration at Guildhall having breakfasted with him at the Mansion House. On the following day the same 16 were to meet for breakfast at 10 a.m. and then proceed 'with the Colours of this Company, Music etc. to Guildhall to meet the Lord Mayor and attend him in procession to the water side'. The Clerk was to see that sufficient coaches were on hand and Mr. Corrock was to 'furnish the Gentlemen with proper Gowns for the two days'. Mr. Rowed (of the *Globe Tavern*) attended and confirmed that he could accommodate 150 people in one room and 40 in another. He produced menus priced at 3s. 0d., 3s. 6d. and 4s. 0d. per head respectively, but the minutes do not say which one was chosen.

Further orders followed. Mr. Simpson was ordered 'to provide two new Colours, one with the Arms of the late Mr. Alderman Burnell and the other with the Arms of the Right Honourable the Lord Mayor elect'. Mr. Cotton was instructed to provide four clarinets, two horns, two bassoons, one trumpet and one bass drum. The musicians were to attend the Mayoral procession and afterwards play to the livery during dinner. Finally, Mr. Spencer of the London Assurance Office was to attend as Bargemaster and he was to provide suitable people to carry the colours.

In due course, the Master, Mr. Eamonson, and 15 others of the livery breakfasted with the Lord Mayor at the Mansion House at 12 noon. Then they went by coach to Guildhall and stood at his left hand during the time of his being sworn into office. Thereafter, they returned to the Mansion House for dinner.

On the following day the 16 met for breakfast at the *George and Vulture Tavern*, Cornhill. Then they went 'with Music and Colours flying and attended by one of the City Marshalls' to Guildhall where they joined the Lord Mayor in procession and attended him to 'the

---

[11] Guildhall Library MS 4591.

15   Sir William Anderson, Lord Mayor 1797

three Cranes'. The Lord Mayor then embarked on board the City barge for Westminster. The 16 liverymen adjourned to *Varley's Hotel* to await his Lordship's return and afterwards they went with him to Guildhall and from there they went, in due course, to the *Globe Tavern* for dinner.

In the following November a similar procedure was followed when a new Lord Mayor took office but on this occasion the 16 stood at Alderman Anderson's right hand.

It is impossible to refrain from comparing the Company's treatment of Alderman Anderson with its treatment of Alderman Burnell. It cannot have been entirely due to questions of expense that the Court appears to have behaved more generously in 1797 than in 1787. The Company's financial position had not improved in the meantime. In fact it had continued to deteriorate. There is no indication in the minutes that Alderman Anderson was asked to contribute towards the costs incurred. Perhaps he was a popular and sympathetic person who attracted the Company's loyalty and support without restraint. Valerie Hope mentions him in unflattering terms in *My Lord Mayor*. He

> cut a comic figure at the royal service of thanksgiving for naval victories in December (1797), when he had to lead the procession on horseback with two grooms holding him on. As a member of parliament he prided himself on his regular attendance but had been absent from a debate at which he had intended to speak, so the current joke was that he had been busy taking riding lessons.[12]

It is highly creditable to the Company that it provided three Lord Mayors within the space of 50 years and that it continued to attract men of ability despite the fact that in general social terms it had so little to offer. Indeed it is creditable that so many new freemen and liverymen were admitted to the Company over the period examined. Throughout that time the Company also provided a strong presence on the Court of Common Council. In the five years 1772, 1779, 1784, 1785 and 1801 the Glovers who were members of the Common Council numbered 6, 11, 11, 10 and 7 respectively. Despite the fact that the number of Councillors was greater then than subsequently, that was a fair representation. It included John Popplewell (Master in 1780), Richard Draper (Master in 1781), Benjamin Robertson (Master in 1783), William Wryghte (Master in 1785), John Hemans (Master in 1786), Christopher Parker (Master in 1789), John Rowlatt (Master in

---

[12]   Hope, *My Lord Mayor*, p.133.

1795) and Joseph Hibbert (Master in 1800). It also included Richard Welch, Sheriff in 1802.

The Minute Books continue until 1804 and the Register of Admissions continues, interestingly, until 1851 by which time the movement for municipal reform was a major concern in the City and the livery companies were being looked at with a fresh perspective. Seen by many as an obstacle to progress and as outdated in their usefulness they were thrown upon the defensive. Tantalisingly, it is just as this new concern about the rights and responsibilities of the livery companies, and particularly their function and role in the government of the City, comes to the fore that the records of the Company are completely absent. There are no Court minutes surviving for the period from 1804 to 1941, an interval of 137 years, and the history and activities of the Company during that time can only be gleaned from sources outside the Company.

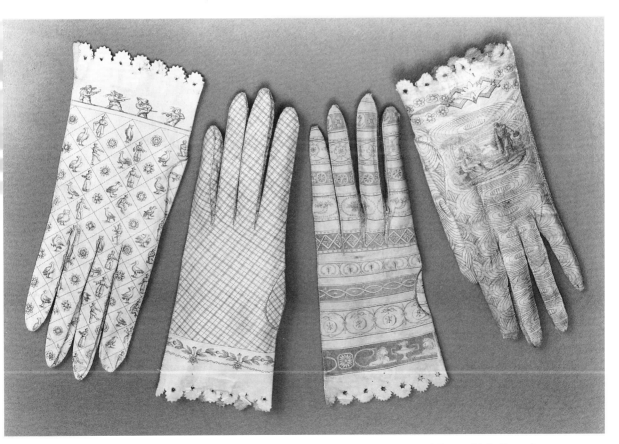

16   Gloves of white kid of the period *c.*1800 variously printed with motifs of leaves and flowers, birds, figures in a landscape with neo-classical designs.

XIV

Pressure for Reform

THE COMPANY's Register of Freedom Admissions shows that in the first half of the 19th century the numbers of admissions are less than those appearing 50 years earlier. In 1832, the year of the Reform Act, the number of new freemen was seven. Ten years later it was four and in the last three years of the Register, for 1849, 1850 and 1851, it was respectively five, two and one. The names include Edward and George Hibbert, free in 1839 and 1851 respectively. Edward Hibbert was Master on three occasions and George Hibbert was Master in 1869/70, 1872/3 and 1874/5 and for no less than 10 years from 1876/7 to 1885/6. Members of the Hibbert family continued to appear in the livery lists down to the 1930s.

Parliamentary reform was followed by municipal reform. In 1833 a Royal Commission was appointed to 'inquire into the existing state of the Municipal Corporations in England and Wales and to collect information respecting the defects in their constitution'. The report which the Commissioners produced dealt with all the corporations except for London itself which was the subject of a separate enquiry, the result of which was published in 1837.[1] It is of particular value in examining the history of the Glovers' Company since, in the course of their work, the Commissioners looked at the role of the livery companies and recorded all the facts they could obtain about their government, their property, their membership and function. Some companies refused to cooperate with the Commissioners, but, fortunately, the Glovers did and so the Report provides much information about the Company in the 1830s.

Mr. R. Thomas of Fen Court, Fenchurch Street, was clerk. He appears on a list of Companies and Clerks in the Corporation of London Record Office in 1832.[2] That year he wrote:

> I beg leave to certify that the present freemen of the Company of Glovers is 307 of whom 168 are of the livery but the Company do not know the residences of about 89 of such freemen, 30 of whom are upon the livery and they believe most of those to be dead.[3]

It appears therefore that the Company remained in a numerically healthy state. Other returns made at that time show the contrasting numbers of Goldsmiths and Horners. The Goldsmiths returned 1,810 freemen and 190 liverymen making 2,000 in all. The Horners returned 14 freemen and no liverymen.[4]

The report of 1837 reveals that no Company except the Carmen was then exclusively composed of persons belonging to the trade from which the Company took its name, and,

---

[1] Report of the Royal Commission on Municipal Corporations (England & Wales) London and Southwark; London Companies [Parly. papers (cmd 239) 1837 xxv].
[2] CLRO Companies 10.14.   [3] CLRO Companies 3.5.   [4] CLRO Companies 10.17.

apart from the Apothecaries, in few of them was the majority so comprised. The Glovers were ranked the 62nd company of the 89 listed, all but four of which were livery companies.

The title of the Company and its Charter with its salient points are recited. Then the ordinances of 1681 are referred to and the resolution of 28 April 1774 establishing an unlimited livery is set out. There follow several passages detailing the workings of the Company.

Females may be members. Six were admitted by redemption between 1780 and 1802. The fees payable on admission to the freedom are £1 payable to the Company, 5s. 6d. payable to the Clerk and 1s. 0d. to the Beadle. Quarterage amounted to 4s. 0d. per annum. No steps were taken to compel those becoming free of the Company to become free of the City.

It was formerly customary to elect Stewards who paid a fine of £10 for the expenses of providing a dinner for the livery on Lord Mayor's Day but such meetings had ceased to be held since 1797. They were discontinued because of the expense to the Stewards by whose fines the expense was paid.

The Company had no hall. Liverymen elected to the Court could pay a fine of £21 which excused them from all offices. The duties of the Court were principally confined to the management of the finances of the Company and to giving donations to poor freemen and liverymen and annuities to poor liverymen's wives. The Court usually sat for two or three hours.

None of the powers given by charter or otherwise over the glove trade were then exercised.

The Company possessed no estates. Its income came solely from fines, fees and quarterage. There were two investments: £1,800 3% Consols and £1,250 Reduced Stock. The dividends were applied firstly towards the general purposes of the Company and thereafter for donations to poor freemen etc.

When anyone applied to purchase the freedom of the Company no notice was given and no proposer and seconder was required. No canvas was made. In the last 30 years no one had been refused the freedom. The fee of £1 on admission had stood at least since 1700. The stamp duty payable was £6 6s. 6d.

Freedom by gift was made rarely. The last occasion was in 1799 when Captain Sir Edward Berry was honoured for services at the Battle of the Nile.[5]

Freemen were usually asked to take up the livery after five years. If a freeman refused he could be fined but no one ever was. The fee on taking up the livery was £10 0s. 0d. There were then about 140 liverymen.

From 1801 to 1833 usually up to 10 liverymen a year were admitted but in 1804 there were 25 and a comparable number of freemen. Mr. Thomas thought they were fairly divided between those arriving by patrimony, by apprenticeship and by redemption. It was calculated that from 1794 to 1833 the records of all freedom admissions in the City showed that 7,794 had been admitted by patrimony, 18,900 by servitude and 13,474 by redemption. Only 53 had been made free by honorary grant.

---

[5] See Chapter XII.

By patrimony all the children, male or female, of a freeman were entitled to the freedom. By apprenticeship you took the Company of your master and not the Company of his trade. If an apprentice transferred to another master he still took the Company of his original master. Widows having freedom by courtesy could take over their husband's apprentices but not if they remarried. Freewomen could take apprentices, their freedom being suspended during coverture.[6]

Freedom by redemption commonly occurred in four different circumstances: where there had been a breach of the apprenticeship (as by serving less than seven years or by marriage during the term); where the applicant wished to be admitted to a company other than that to which he would otherwise be entitled; by grace and favour, and finally by presentment of the Chamberlain or some other person entitled to grant the freedom.

In 1840, Mr. Thomas was still Clerk. He compiled a list of those liverymen entitled to vote in the election of the City's Members of Parliament. Such liverymen had to live in the City or within seven miles thereof.[7] The number of Glovers who qualified to vote was one hundred and thirty-three.[8]

Five years later, in 1845, Mr. Thomas made another return to the City authorities. He revealed that 34 freemen lived within the City and 75 lived outside it, and that 21 liverymen lived in the City with 79 living out of it but all within a seven-mile radius.[9] The figures are interesting in that they reveal the movement to the suburbs of the majority of the freemen and liverymen.

Again in 1852 Mr. Thomas made a further return of those liverymen eligible to vote for the City's members of parliament. He revealed that 78 were entitled to vote and 15 were not. There were 105 freemen in the Company and in the last seven years 17 freemen and six liverymen had been admitted.[10]

In 1866 the companies were required to make a return of the number of liverymen disqualified from voting for Members of Parliament by reason of the residential qualification. Sixty-three companies made returns but they did not include the Glovers. Some companies were showing signs of becoming moribund. One clerk wrote of his liverymen '… with few exceptions most of them are quite lost sight of and I am unable to say whether they are alive or dead. Therefore it is quite impossible to make an accurate return'.[11]

Many of the companies were now struggling to survive. The agitation for the reform of the City administration continued and showed no sign of diminishing. From time to time the livery companies as constituents of the Corporation came under scrutiny. They were widely perceived to be an anachronism performing no useful function, divorced from the real commerce and trade of the country, providing their members with a lavish

---

[6] The condition of a woman during marriage she being then under the cover, influence and protection of her husband. Married women became admissible to the freedom of the City in 1923 (CLRO Minutes of proceedings of the Court of Common Council 1923, p.116).

[7] An Act of 1867 extended the residential limit to 25 miles of the City limits. However, the Representation of the People Act 1918 sect. 17(1) abolished the right of liverymen as such to exercise the parliamentary franchise in the City but permitted those who possessed a business qualification to be entered on a separate list of liverymen in the register of parliamentary electors and to vote at Guildhall. In 1947 this special register contained 740 names. Jones, *The Corporation of London*, p.15. The Representation of the People Act 1948 abolished the business premises qualification and it abolished the separate parliamentary constituency of the City of London uniting it with the City of Westminster to form one constituency.

[8] CLRO Companies 11.1.   [9] CLRO Companies 10.9.   [10] CLRO Companies Box 1.1.

[11] CLRO Companies Box 1.2.

and selfish form of hospitality, and totally without merit in their civic privileges.

Already in the 1830s the Corporation had reduced the size of the freedom fine and Common Council had resolved that it was no longer necessary for a freeman to belong to a company. As Dr. I.G. Doolittle explains,[12] 'the threat to the livery franchise, the dismantlement of the freedom regulations, the severance of contact with the trades, declining interest in the civic life of Guildhall', all tended to undermine the morale of the livery. The lesser companies had very little to offer their members other than the right to vote in Common Hall if they were on the livery. Perhaps the fact that Mr. George Hibbert should serve as Master for 13 years, no less than 10 of them in succession, is evidence that the Glovers were, like others, in decline. That was not

17 Sir Henry Homewood Crawford, five times Master of the Company.

all, however. In the eight years from 1877/8 to 1884/5 not only did the Master continue in office but he was supported by the same Wardens now reduced to two in number, and in the years 1885/6 and 1886/7 there were no Wardens at all appointed, seeming thereby to indicate a terminal state of decline.

In 1884, another Royal Commission reported on the state of the livery companies.[13] By then 13 companies were said to be extinct, although three of them (the Gardeners, the Paviors and the Tobacco Pipe Makers) survived. A very full return of information was required from the companies. They were asked to give the date of foundation of the company and the circumstances of its origin; the charters and similar instruments in the possession of the company should be listed and an abstract of each provided; details should be given of any trust deeds; lists and details of decrees of any Court (whether Courts of Law or the Court of Aldermen or of Common Council) should be given; a list and abstract of any other documents which affected the company should be produced; a concise history of the company, its objects and how far they had been carried out was required, the question was raised whether the company had any licence in mortmain[14] and, if so, to what extent and, in addition, whether the company had any control over any art, trade or business and, if so, how was such control constituted. Finally, the companies were asked to list their charities and to give full details of them and to say how the charitable funds had been applied over the last ten years.

---

[12] Doolittle, *The City of London*, p.89.
[13] Report of the Royal Commission on the City of London Livery Companies [Parly. papers (cmd 4037) 1884 xxxix].
[14] Literally 'dead hand'; such a state of possession of land as made it deemed inalienable, as when land was transferred to religious houses or corporations. For such a transfer licence from the Crown or, later, Parliament was required.

The Glovers made no return of this information. They were not alone although most companies complied. On 15 February 1882 the Secretary of the Commissioners wrote to the Clerk asking him 'to draw to the attention of the Court of the Worshipful Company of Glovers the fact that, tho' about one and a half years had elapsed since the Commissioners' request for information, they had not yet had the honour to receive any information from the Court'.

They desired him to add 'that they regretted the delay and asked to be informed within one month whether the Court intended to send in returns and at what date the Commissioners may expect to receive them'.

By this time the Company had a new clerk, Mr. F.R. Thomas of 85 Gracechurch Street. On 9 March he replied:

> I have to acknowledge your letter of the 15th ultimo and in reply have to refer you to my letter of the 6th September last [a letter stating that the Company declined to make returns].
>
>   The funds possessed by the Glovers' Company consist of £2000 Consols and £1800 Reduced Stock.

A measure of the vast difference in wealth between the major and the minor companies may be gauged by comparing the size of the Glovers' investments with the total wealth of the livery companies which was estimated at £15 million. Their income was calculated to be (for 1879/80) £750,000 to £800,000 a year, of which £200,000 was specifically committed to charitable causes.[15]

A list[16] survives of the liverymen of the Company entitled to vote in 1886 for the election of Members of Parliament for the City. The list includes three members of the Hibbert family including George Hibbert, the Master, and a number of future Masters including Henry Homewood Crawford, the City solicitor, Master for three years from 1886 to 1889 and again in 1898 and 1905, and Mr. John Charles Bell who subsequently (as Sir John Bell) became Lord Mayor in 1907. The total number was forty-nine.

It cannot have been a sign of well-being that two Masters should have officiated between them for 16 years. Dr. Doolittle points to the 1870s as a time of revival of the livery companies. In the case of the smaller companies he remarks that[17] often they owed the stimulus to their change of fortunes to one man. He mentions Sir Homewood Crawford's efforts for the Fanmakers. But it seems likely that the Glovers' Company also owed a great deal to his efforts. His appointment as Master in 1886 brought the long rule of George Hibbert to an end. He seems to have at once revitalised the Company. Four new Wardens were appointed and a new Clerk took over from Mr. F.R. Thomas. Sir Homewood Crawford is said to have been instrumental in obtaining the Company's Inspeximus Charter granted by Queen Victoria on 21 March 1898 which ratified and

---

[15] See Report of the Royal Commission on the City of London Livery Companies 1884.
[16] CLRO Companies 11.2.
[17] Doolittle, *The City of London*, p.89.

18 Victorian silver gilt rosewater dish presented by Henry Homewood Crawford, 1899.

19 Victorian large chased flagon and cover presented by Alfred Moseley, 1913-14.

confirmed the original charter.[18] He was undoubtedly assisted in his efforts to revive the Company by that other renowned defender of the livery, Benjamin Scott, the City Chamberlain, who had been admitted to the freedom of the Company as long ago as 22 December 1841. Benjamin Scott served as a Warden in 1891/2. It was reported that he 'had close personal as well as professional links with the livery companies' and that he 'did much to promote the revival of the Glovers' Company of which he was a freeman by patrimony and became one of the Court of Assistants'.[19] He presented to the Company the Beadle's staff now in use.[20] Over and above this, and since no individual could single-handedly revive a company's flagging fortunes, Dr. Doolittle suggests that the unceasing attention of the reformers had had a perverse effect. The citizens of London had looked again at these ancient institutions and decided that they were worthy of their support and not wholesale reform or abolition.[21]

In 1887 the City of London Ballot Act required that clerks of companies prepare a yearly list of those entitled to vote at Common Hall.[22] For the year 1887/8 the number of Glovers so entitled was twenty-nine. That was a low point from which the Company grew steadily. By 1897/8 the number of liverymen was seventy-five. By way of comparison it may be noted that the Haberdashers numbered 438, the Spectacle Makers 334, and the Merchant Taylors two hundred and seventy-four. At the other end of the scale the Woolmen numbered 20, the Bowyers 19, the Fletchers 12 and the Carmen four. The livery of the Glovers' Company did not vary much up to the First World War. Generally speaking, the total remained in the seventies and in 1912/13 it was eighty.[23]

It is disappointing that no minutes or other records of the Company survive to show its progress during the first 40 years of the present century up to the outbreak of the Second World War. We do know, however, from the statistics supplied by the Clerk[24] that the number of those entitled to vote at Common Hall, i.e. the livery, steadily increased. In 1917 it numbered seventy-seven. By 1922/23 the number had grown to 88 and five years later it was one hundred and eight. By 1932/33 the number was 113, a number sustained until the outbreak of war.

During the first 40 years of this century two more Lord Mayors came from the ranks of the Glovers' Company. The first, Sir John Charles Bell, Lord Mayor in 1907, was Master of the Company for the three years 1892/3, 1899/1900 and 1907/8. He was a Glover but his mother company was the Fanmakers. Then, in 1933, Sir Charles Collett served both as Lord Mayor and Master of the Company.

---

[18]   Colonel Robert J. Blackham, *London's Livery Companies* (London, n.d.) at p.304 says that 'litigation with the Crown was brought to an amicable conclusion and Queen Victoria granted the Company a new charter confirming … the original Stuart document' and Peter Lawson-Clarke in his *Brief History of the Worshipful Company of Glovers* (1982) mentions that there had been a dispute with the Treasury which, fortunately, was settled about this time. Sir Homewood Crawford was presented with a handsome tea-tray by the Company in 1899 for his services. The tray is now in the Company's possession having been purchased in 1938.

[19]   Betty R. Masters, *The Chamberlain of the City of London 1287-1987* (London, 1988).

[20]   An unexpected pleasure arising out of the preparation of this history was to find myself in correspondence with a collateral descendant of Benjamin Scott. Mr. John William Scott informed me that his great-great-great-grandfather, John Scott, was in 1769 apprenticed to James Duppa of 15 Aldgate, goldsmith and jeweller, a citizen and Glover of London. John Scott's eldest son also came into the freedom in 1819. He was Mr. J.W. Scott's ancestor. It was from a second son, also a Glover, that Benjamin Scott was descended.

[21]   Doolittle, *The City of London*, p.91.

[22]   Prior to this the position was governed by the City of London Election Act 1725 under which the Companies were obliged to make a list when required by the Lord Mayor.

[23]   These figures are taken from CLRO Companies Box 584A.   [24]   ibid.

Epilogue

THE ROMAN GOD, Janus, is depicted facing both ways. He looks both behind and before him. He was the guardian of the gateway, and as the Company stands poised before the millennium it is, perhaps, appropriate to look back at the centuries which have passed and then, pausing to examine the present, to turn to face the future.

The previous chapters have shown that for a long time throughout the late Middle Ages the Company consisted of a small group bound together by a shared occupation and the shared act of religious worship; then the religious element declined and as the gloving industry expanded the dominant concern became the need to preserve standards, and to protect the quality of the materials used and the reputation of the craft. In time those matters in turn ceased to engage the Company's attention. Long ago the time came when the industry became centred elsewhere than in London and the Company ceased to represent working glovers. Other and various occupations far removed from gloving occupied the livery and all pretence at control of the craft ceased. The Company was a company of glovers in name though not in fact.

Eventually, a sort of mundane regularity seems to have prevailed. The bye-laws provided a framework for the appointment of the ruling body, enabling a form of government to continue, and with no great issues to excite controversy the Court of Assistants concerned itself with matters of routine interest.

As we have seen, the Company seems always to have been able to attract a steady supply of freemen, at any rate until the 19th century when admission by apprenticeship began to wane and the livery was similarly maintained. However the 19th century, which began quietly enough for the livery companies, soon produced enormous changes. It can be argued that the London companies were fortunate to be excluded from the provisions of the Municipal Corporations Act 1835. Elsewhere, the provincial companies lost their power to grant the freedom by redemption and they lost their exclusive trading rights and their freedom from tolls and their right to choose from their members the administrators of the boroughs they represented. It is true that they had long been in decline but thereafter those few which survived did so for particular reasons; they owned property or administered charitable trusts or became rather exclusive dining clubs. In London the time of trial came later when the press and public opinion turned against these bodies which were widely seen as outdated and effete. They were accused of being wealthy and undemocratic, an anachronism in a modernising age. It was fortunate that there were those who guided the Company through those difficult years.

It has to be said that the 20th century seems to have begun as very much a continuation of what went before. In the absence of any minutes showing the activity of the Court of Assistants in the first 40 years one cannot be certain but it seems probable that the nature of the business transacted cannot have been very different from that which occupied the Court 100 years previously.

After an interval of over 100 years the Minute Books begin again in July 1941 and the Court of Assistants continued to meet to transact business throughout the War. It is apparent that the Company was a casualty of the enemy air raids. There is a reference to 'the destruction of the Company's records at Bastien House'[1] and the Master's badge of office was lost and the Company's seal destroyed.

Most significantly, the first steps to rebuild the links between the Company and the glove trade were tentatively taken. In 1943 Mr. Watson Humphries recalled that before the War a committee was appointed to arrange a Glovers' Week and to cooperate generally with the industry as a whole. In 1941 the death of Past Master Whitby was reported. He was 'the father of the glove trade' and had brought the trade into closer association with the Company. Those links were to continue. Occasionally there were setbacks, as when a scheme to provide diplomas and medals to the best apprentices at the Glove Cutting School at Yeovil ran into difficulties, apparently because of trade union concerns.

In 1943 the assets of the Company had risen to the sum of £6,400. There was no charitable fund as such. Payments might be made on an *ad hoc* basis from the general funds.

From time to time items of particular interest occur. In 1948, Mr. Frederick Giles, Master that year, presented some white gloves and gauntlets to be worn by the Master on ceremonial occasions. In 1952 four banners bearing the arms of former liverymen were discovered at Apothecaries' Hall and handed over to the Company.[2] In 1955 the Company formally resolved to adopt the 21st SAS Regiment (Artists Rifles) TA. In 1953 the Company was granted the honour by the Lord Chancellor's Office of providing the Coronation Glove for Queen Elizabeth. Curiously, long afterwards, in 1968, the Company became involved in a claim by a Frenchman, the Marquis of Verdun, who said he had an interest in the glove as a descendant of Bertram of Verdun. Apparently Bertram had been granted the right to provide the glove by William the Conqueror and the Marquis requested a replica. His request was refused.

In 1956, Sotheby's sold a King James II tankard commemorating Mr. Walter Thomas, Master of the Company in 1687. Unfortunately, the funds of the Company did not permit the Court to contemplate buying it.

At the close of the decade, in 1959, came the momentous gift by Mr. Robert Spence of his collection of historic gloves now housed at the Museum of Costume at Bath. There are some 125 pairs of decorative gloves and the collection covers British glove making of the period from the late 16th century until the middle of the 19th century. It is deemed one of the finest collections of its kind both in this country and throughout the world. As well as gloves richly embroidered and employing popular motifs of flowers, leaves, birds and beasts, and sometimes allegories such as the story of Jonah and the whale, the collection includes a number of gloves of Italian and Spanish origin. That gift has proved of enormous significance and is a source of great pride to the livery.

---

[1] Perhaps this accounts for the loss of many of the Company's records.
[2] The arms are those of Sir Homewood Crawford, Major Joseph, an Assistant, William Alpheus Higgs, Sheriff of London 1887/8, an Assistant, and Major E. Pugh, VC, a liveryman.

However, looked at dispassionately, the great days of the Company seem to have been those of the Elizabethan period and continuing up to the outbreak of the Civil War. The Glovers are shown to have been argumentative and disputatious. They behaved as if full of confidence in their rightness in all things. They are audacious, persistent, resourceful and difficult. Above all they believed they had a just cause and they were prepared to persevere until they achieved their goals. It cannot have been a coincidence that the same period represented a high point in the quality of their workmanship and the beauty and elegance of the gloves they produced. They have been described as 'high fashion items intended more for display and ceremonial use than for everyday wear … gauntlet gloves lavishly embroidered with multi-coloured silks and seed pearls, trimmed with metallic lace and spangled or decorated with looped and ruched ribbons'.[3]

Creative activity went side by side with the vigorous pursuit of the Glovers' quest to control their industry through the search and sealing of tawed leather. As Past Master John Gratwick put it,[4] 'the changes in fashion which occurred during the reign of Elizabeth I and in the early 17th century allowed the Glovers to prosper'.

Now, in the late 20th century they have begun to prosper again.

In *The City of London and its Livery Companies*, Dr. Doolittle quotes the opinion of a company historian that the 1870s saw 'the great awakening' of the livery companies from their prolonged lethargy. In the case of the Glovers' Company it may be shown that in the following decade it acquired fresh impetus, but it was not until 100 years later that anything approaching 'a great awakening' took place.

By the 1960s the Company was in evident need of reform on several grounds.[5] There were stirrings of unrest because of the almost complete lack of involvement by members of the livery, at any rate those outside the Court of Assistants, in the affairs of the Company. Liverymen had no means of getting to know each other and had no knowledge of the organisation and workings of the Company. The only communications they received were the formal City Summonses for the election of the Lord Mayor and Sheriff, the invitation to the United Guilds Service and to the annual banquet at the Mansion House. Indeed, liverymen did not even know the name of their Master until they received their invitations to the banquet towards the end of the Master's year of office. The Court met four times a year and then lunched together. There were no other meetings of any kind.

It is true that the Court was aware that such a state of affairs was unsatisfactory and it was a matter of concern for three decades how best to rectify the matter. As Past Master Heard put it in 1951, 'the Court should consider some method of liaison between the Court and the members of the livery by which the latter may be kept informed of the Company's activities and an opportunity offered for discussion with the livery in regard to the affairs of the Company'.[6] The same year a Ladies' Dinner was held in April[7] in addition to the annual banquet in October. It was felt that regular livery dinners following

---

[3] Penelope Ruddock, Curator of the Museum of Costume, Bath.
[4] In the Glovers' Company Handbook.
[5] I am greatly indebted to Past Master Sir Christopher Collett, GBE, for much of the information resulting from 'the great awakening'.
[6] See the Minutes of the Court of Assistants, 1 November 1951, Guildhall Library MS. 4591/6.
[7] At Cutlers' Hall. It was a success but the experiment was not continued.

Court meetings would not be sufficiently well supported. Throughout those post-war years it is evident that the Court was exercised to find ways of increasing contact with the livery but no satisfactory formula was reached. It was a general problem evidenced by the fact that the Lord Mayor[8] put out the suggestion that companies should stimulate interest by inviting the livery to attend Court luncheons and dinners.

The Company's financial position had not improved to any extent and faced with the spectre of inflation it was likely to deteriorate. The only income received continued to be from fines and fees. Liverymen paid a sum on admission and on advancement to the Court and to higher office but they did not pay quarterage. Consequently, to maintain any semblance of stability it was necessary to have a steady supply of new members. Nevertheless, since liverymen were not supplied with any financial information they remained in ignorance of the true position.

Moreover, despite the promising beginnings of revived links with the glove trade made in earlier years, contact with the trade remained rather distant and impersonal. The Master might occasionally attend a lunch or dinner or make a trade presentation and he made an annual presentation of a prize at Leathersellers' College at Northampton but that was the extent of the Company's involvement.

The Spence collection of gloves which had been housed in the Museum of London for security had had no provision made for its restoration or conservation. The livery were not encouraged to visit or take an interest in it and students of fashion had little opportunity of consulting it.

No attempt was made to educate the livery in the traditions of the City or to encourage members to attend and support the election of the Lord Mayor and Sheriffs as was their right and duty. The Lord Mayor and Lady Mayoress were presented with gloves at a lunch in January but the event was attended only by members of the Court and their ladies. Perhaps most significantly there was hardly any involvement with the public at large. In 1954 the Court had decided that it was not practicable to set up a charitable fund except as a long-term policy. They did not consider that individual liverymen should be asked to subscribe. They recommended that a fund be set up by putting aside 10 per cent of any available surplus of income each year to be used for liverymen or their dependants in need of *ex gratia* payment; for charitable objects associated with the City, the livery companies and the Lord Mayor's appeal; for charitable objects associated with the livery of the Company or the trade, and lastly for charities generally on the special recommendation of the Court. There was no separate charitable fund and occasional donations were made, most commonly out of the pockets of members of the Court, of sums not exceeding £100 in any year.

Fortunately, all these problems came to be addressed and those who recognised the dangers are to be congratulated for their foresight. Two separate working parties were appointed to consider what reforms should be made over the whole field of activity of the Company. The first, under the chairmanship of Past Master James Birkmyre Rowan, reported in 1970 and the second, under Past Master Clifford Henry Barclay, reported in

---

[8] Reported in the minutes of the Court of Assistants, 18 April 1961, Guildhall Library MS 4591/7.

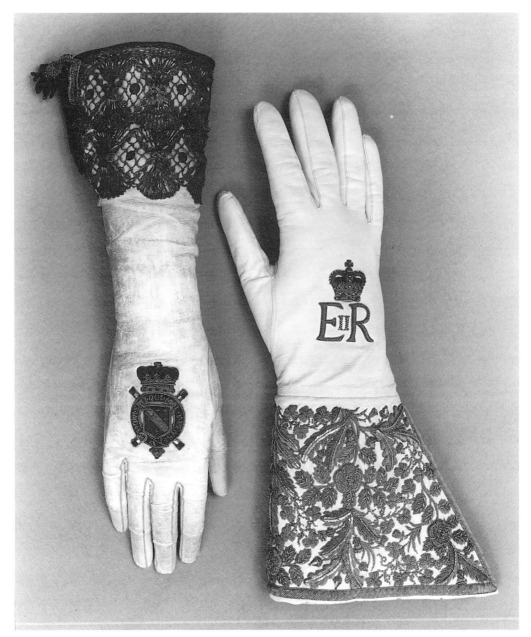

20 An elbow length glove of white kid lined with crimson satin made for Queen Victoria. The garter emblem and crown embroidered decorate the back of the hand. Also the original coronation glove of Queen Elizabeth II. The Queen's cypher replaces the previous coat of arms.

1977. As a result of their recommendations and of further and consequential reforms since put in place it is fair to say that the prospects of the Company have been transformed.

Gone are the days when the livery might feel they were ignored. The administration of the Company has been broadened to reflect the increased activity in which members of the Company are encouraged to participate. Such administration is largely in the hands of new committees which have been created and which consequently relieve the burden which would otherwise fall on the Court of Assistants and, as the committees are largely manned by ordinary liverymen and women, more and more people become involved in and are made aware of the workings of the Company.

There are new opportunities for promotion to the Court since each year a vacancy is created by the departure of the senior Past Master who then becomes an honorary Court member and promotion is no longer seen to be simply a matter of seniority. Those who wish to progress in the Company now have an opportunity to do so and to be identified as suitable for invitation to join the Court.

Members of the livery are now present at lunch in January when gloves are presented to the Lord Mayor and Lady Mayoress and they are present when the new Master and Wardens are installed later in the year. Nowadays, many other functions are arranged which enable the livery to meet and get to know each other. The Company produces a Newsletter which is circulated to members and livery lists are sent to members each year. Masters invariably make every effort to become widely known within the livery and the engagements they undertake increase year by year.

Through one of the Company's committees liverymen are encouraged to attend not only the elections of the Lord Mayor and the Sheriffs but also the Lord Mayor's Show and the United Guilds Service and after the elections a lunch is organised at which a speaker on a City subject gives a short address. New liverymen are instructed about the aims and objects of a livery company and about their obligations to the City. The Company took part in the Lord Mayor's Shows in 1980 and 1989, the first occasions since 1933, and the Company routinely supports the City's charitable projects as, for example, the biennial Red Cross Fair.

Collaboration and co-operation with the glove trade has expanded. A Glove Trade liaison committee has been established. Awards are made to organisations and individuals who have substantially benefited the industry and to students of glove design. Long service certificates are presented to those who have been working glovers for over 25 years and special presentations of gloves are made from time to time as on the occasion of the engagement of members of the Royal Family.

The Spence collection of gloves, which had languished in comparative obscurity, was enhanced by the gift by Messrs. Harborow, formerly of New Bond Street, of their duplicate series of Royal gloves. That company for 150 years had the privilege of providing the right hand glove traditionally presented to the sovereign on his or her coronation and a duplicate was always held in reserve in case of accident. The Company of Glovers now has a policy of restoring and conserving its collections and of building up a new collection of fashion gloves to cover the period from 1860 onwards as a modern addition to Robert Spence's gift. The Company has established a separate charity to care for its collections and to advance public education in the historical, social and artistic value of gloves. Its aim is to make the collections available for public display and to award, in suitable cases, grants of scholarships to students to enable them to research this valuable archive.

The Company's finances have been regularised through careful management and the re-introduction of quarterage payments. Moreover, a charitable trust was formed in

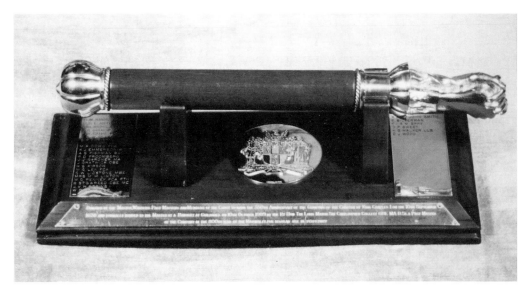

21 Mace presented by the Master, Wardens, Past Wardens and members of the Court to mark the 350th anniversary of the granting of the Charter by King Charles I.

22 The Master, Wardens and past and present members of the Court of Assistants, July 1999. 1. F.W. Caine, 2. H.S. Kirsch, 3. C.J. Wood, 4. D.P.L. Antill, 5. H.G. Simon, 6. B.M.V. Bovey, 7. C.W. Lidstone, 8. D.P. Sweet, 9. J.L. Hewitt, 10. J.H. Spanner (Third Under Warden), 11. V. Maddox (Beadle), 12. K.D. St J. Smith, 13. A.S. Fishman, 14. B. St G. A. Reed, 15. H.R. Beakbane, 16. D.M. Anderson, 17. P. Lawson Clarke (former Clerk), 18. M.K. Down, 19. L.M. Harvey, 20. W. Loach, 21. A. Howarth (Second Under Warden), 22. J.D.H. Clarke (First Under Warden), 23. M. Silverman, 24. F.I.R.M. Spry, 25. Mrs. M. Hood (Clerk), 26. M.S. Lea, 27. M.O. Penney (Master), 28. J.R. Clayton, 29. Mrs. M.M. Linton (Renter Warden).

1975 when a separate charitable fund was established. It has quickly grown. Its objects are to raise funds in order to make grants and carry out projects which, so far as is possible, involve the provision of gloves. Preference is given to grants and projects for the welfare of the glove trade and its employees and pensioners, for education, for the disabled and for all disadvantaged members of society, particularly those connected with the City of London.

In 1979, in tune with the spirit of the times, ladies were admitted to the livery and 20 years later the Company expects to install its first lady Master, Mrs. Margaret Mavis Linton.[9] Looking to the future, the Company introduced a category of associate membership in 1981 so that overseas members of the glove trade and others might be introduced into the Company. In course of time, as new legislation appears, they may acquire full livery status. Typical of the Company's outgoing approach was the decision to investigate the possibility of forming links with European guilds which has resulted in reciprocal visits with the Safron Guild of Basel. Their black and silver band enlivened the Company's float in the 1989 Lord Mayor's Show.

There has been much to celebrate. In 1989 the 350th anniversary of the granting of the Company's Charter was commemorated and, by a happy coincidence, the City marked the 800th anniversary year of the Mayoralty. That year the Lord Mayor of London was Sir Christopher Collett, GBE, himself a former Master of the Glovers' Company who followed in the footsteps of his grandfather, Sir Charles Collett, who was both Lord Mayor and Master of the Company in 1933.

The Glovers' Company has no portraits or descriptions to give flesh and authenticity to the generations who have gone before; none that is until 1962. In that year Mr. Wilfred Ernest Palmer MBE was Master, and he died, tragically, during his year of office in St Paul's Cathedral, before the commencement of the annual United Guilds Service. Mr. Victor Morley Lawson, then the Third Under Warden, who was present, wrote a dignified and moving description of the event and of the Master so that we might know what kind of man he was. That account, which forms Appendix VII, described a competent intelligent man, rather precise of manner but polite, friendly and considerate, 'regarded by his brethren with esteem and affection' who must serve as a model for all.

The Company of Glovers remains, as it began, a fellowship in which the ties of hospitality and friendship are recognised and valued. It has learned the wisdom of self-examination and the need to have regard to the wider public needs and attitudes. Now it has a purpose. It attracts the support of an informed livery. It serves the community and the glove trade and it supports the City of London. The Company faces the future in good heart, modern in outlook, but retaining the good manners and usages of its historic inheritance.

---

[9]   The first woman Master of a livery company was elected in 1983 in the Chartered Secretaries' Company. *City of London Directory and Livery Companies Guide*, 1984, p.128.

APPENDIX I

Ordinances of the Glovers' Company
made in the year 1349

These are the points and Ordinances which the good folks, the Glovers of London, request to have and to hold as firm and established for ever, to the saving of their trade and to the great profit of the common people.

In the first place – that no foreigner in this trade shall keep shop, or shall follow this trade, or sell or buy, if he be not a freeman of the City.

Also that no one of this trade shall be admitted to the freedom of the City without the assent of the Wardens of the same trade, or the greater part thereof.

Also – that no one of this trade shall take or entice the serving man of another away from the service of his master so long as he is bound by covenant to serve him, on pain of paying twenty shillings to the use of the Chamber, if before the Mayor and Aldermen by the people of the said trade he shall be convicted thereof.

Also – that if any servant in the said trade shall make away with the goods or chattels of his master to the value of twelve pence, more or less, the same default shall be redressed by the good folks who are Wardens of the said trade; and if such servant who shall have offended against his master will not allow himself to be adjudged upon by the Wardens of the said trade he shall be forthwith attached, and brought before the Mayor and Aldermen; and before them let the default be punished, according to their discretion.

Also – that no one of them shall sell his wares in any house at night by candle-light; seeing that folks cannot have such good knowledge by candle-light as by day-light; whether the wares are made of good leather or of bad, or whether they are well and lawfully or falsely made; on pain of forfeiting to the use of the Chamber the wares so sold by candle-light.

Also – that if any false work touching the said trade shall be found or brought for sale within the franchise of the said City, it shall be forthwith taken by the Wardens of the said trade and brought before the Mayor and Aldermen; and before them adjudged to be such as it shall be found to be, upon oath of the folks of the said trade.

Also – that all things touching the said trade that are sold between foreigner and foreigner [within the City], shall be forfeited according to the ancient usages of the City.

Also – that every servant of the said trade who works by the day, shall not take more for his labour and work in the trade than he was wont to take two or three years before the time when these points and Ordinances were accepted by Walter Turke, Mayor, and the Aldermen; that is to say the Monday next after the Feast of the Epiphany (6th January) in the twenty third year of the reign of King Edward after the Conquest the Third.

Also – whereas some persons who are not in the said trade, do take and entice unto themselves the servants of folks in the same trade, and set them to work in secret in their houses and make gloves of rotten and bad leather and do sell them wholesale to strange dealers coming into the City, in deceit of the people, and to the great scandal of the good folks of the said trade; that the Wardens of the said trade make search in such manner for gloves made by false material, that the same may be found and brought before the Mayor and Aldermen; and before them let the same be adjudged to be such as they shall be found to be, upon oath of the good folks of the said trade.

Also – if any one of the said trade shall be found to be recalcitrant, and to act against the points aforesaid, or any one point among them, let him be attached by a serjeant of the Chamber at the suit of the Wardens of the said trade, to appear before the Mayor and Aldermen; and before them let him be punished at their discretion.

And be it known that the underwritten were elected by the wiser and wealthier men of the aforesaid mistery to keep the above articles, and were sworn before the Mayor and Aldermen to do so viz Robert de Goldesburgh, Thomas de Gloucestre, John de Norwyche, John le Barber, William de Derby and John de Wodhulle.

APPENDIX II

Articles and Ordynaunces of the
Fraternitie of the Craft of Glovers made in 1354

In the Worshipe of the holy and hye Trinite fadir and sone and holy Goost And in the Worshipe of the blessed and Glorious Virgyne Mary Moder of oure Lord Godde Jhesu Crist Maistres and Kepers or Wardeyns of the Fraternite of the Craft of Glovers of the Cite of London and alle of the same Fraternite brethren with oon consente and assent in the worshipe and solempne festes the Nunciacion and in especiall the Assumpcion of the blessed Mary Virgine they have doon ordeyned and ymade alle the Articles and Ordynaunces undirwrite by hem and either of hem and here successours for evirmore wel and truly to be kepte to be holde and fulfilled upon the peynes in the same Articles here aftir specified.

First it is ordeyned that every brothir of the same Fraternite the which for the tyme beyng and here successors for here tymes paieth or doth to paye yerely to fynde ij, Tapres of the wight everych of hem of x li. wax brenyng in the Chapel of Oure Lady ysette in the Newchirchawe beside London atte the Hye Auter of the same Chapell in the worshipe of the Blessid Virgine Marye xvj d. to be paied that it is to wete every quarter of the yere iiij d. to the fyndyng of the forseid light and to the pore of the same Fraternitee the whiche well and trewly have paied here quarterage as longe as they and to here power have done.

Also it is ordeyned that if any brother of the same Fraternite of the Crafte of Glovers be behynde of paiement of his quarterage by a monyth aftir the ende of any quarter that thanne for defaute of paiement of soch quarterage he shal paie or do to be paied xvj d. st. that is to wete viij d. to the olde werk of the Churche of Seynt Poule of London and other viij d. to the Boxe of the same Fraternitee of the Graft of Glovers And so as oftetymes as it happeth any brothir be behynde in paiement of his quarterage any quarter of the yere or be not obedient to the somounce of the Wardeyns or be not present in the heuenys that folk ben dede and in offerynges for to be doon as in berying of the bodyes of the brethren of the same Fraternitee of Oure Lady that is to wete the Annunciacion and Assumpcion specially and in alle othir tymes in the which brethren of the same Craft of Glovers togedyr owen for to be And that for every defaute he paye xvj d. in maner and forme as is above expressed And that the Maistres Kepers or Wardeyns of the same Fraternitee which for the tyme ben such sommes of money for everych defaute so ygadred shul do to rere or doon to be rered othir elles an othir that the same Maistres Kepers or Wardeyns a fore said for the same defautes of here owen proper godes shal make satisfaccion and yelde accompte ther of the same sommes in the endes of the yeres of thike Kepers or Wardeyns that is for to say as for ij yere.

Also it is ordeyned that every brother of the same Fraternitee shul come to Placebo and Dirige and in the heuenys of dede folk in sute or in here lyverey of the same ffraternite of the yere last passed and in the morowe atte Masse and there for to offer alle suych brethren in here newe lyverey or sute atte suych offerynges for to be doon owen for to be upon the peyne of xvj d. to paie in maner and fourme above seid.

Also it is ordeyned that if ther be any brother of the same Fraternite and of the same Craft of Glovers be behynde of paiement of his quarterage by a yere and a day and his power the same quarterage to paie And if he that do maliciously refuse that thenne he be somened to fore the officiall and by the Wardeyns for his trespas and rebelnes of suche maner duly for to be chastised or ponyssed and to paie the fyne afore seid and her costes of the court as in here account to fore alle othir brethren of the same Craft wellen answere.

Also it is ordeyned that if any brothir or sister of the same Fraternite if have be of the Craft of Glovers and be dede withymme the endes and the lymytees of the citee of London and have not of his owen godes hym for to berye, he shal have abowte his body v. tapres everych of the wight of x lb. bernyng and iiij torches upon the costes and expenses of the brethren of the same Fraternite if it have be that he by vij yere contynuyng in the same Fraternitee so long hath duelled and his quarterage wel and truly aftir his power ypayde.

Also it is ordeyned that alle the brethren of the same Fraternite ben clothed in oon sute onys every ij yere ayeyns the ffeste offe Assumpcion of oure Lady. And that all soch brethren that is to wete of the forseid Crafte of the Werk of Glovers in the same fest of Assumpcion atte the forseid chapell of oure Lady in the Newe Chirchawe beside London ysette for thanne togedir personlich togedir shul neighberly and there here offerynges shul doon as the maner afore hath ben And if any brothir that day be absent but if a cause resonable hym doth lette that thenne for his absens of the same he pay xvj d. for to be paied in maner and fourme above seid.

Also it is ordeyned that the Maistres Kepers and Wardeyns of the Fraternite afore seid of the Craft of Glovers of the Cite of London the which for the tyme shul be and alle othir brethren of the same Fraternite and of the same Craft of Glovers for here tymes in the feste of Assumpcion of the blessyd Virgyne Marie atte the aforeseid Chapell of Oure Lady in the Newe Churchawe beside London ysette personally shul neighe and come by vij of the clokke to fore the oure of ix. And therfore to be in syngyng of masses and ther her offerynges for to do after the maner of longe tyme passed and ther of forto contynue and abyde and remayne from the same oure of vij vnto the our of viij fullich fulfilled but if they have cause resonable hem for to lette upon the peyne of xvj d. to be paied in maner and fourme, aboveseid.

Also it is ordeyned that every brothir of the same Fraternite that is to wete of the Craft of Glovers her lyvery of the same Craft by iiij yere holde next sewyng aftir that he is receyved hole and faire shal it kepe and the same in no maner withynne thike iiij yere shal not leve it ne selle it ne aliene it upon the peyne of xl d. to paie therof xx d. to the olde werk of the Church of Seynt Poule of London and the othir xx d. to the boxe of the Fraternite of the same Craft.

Also it is ordeyned if any brothir of the forseid Fraternite of the Craft of Glovers aforseid absente hym from his mete and he be withynne the Cite of London butte if it be that he holde with grete sikenes or any othir cause resonable hym doth lette that thanne for his absens of the same he shal paie xl. d. that is to wete xx d. to the olde werke of the Churche of Seynt Poule and the other xx d. to the box of the same Fraternite.

Also it is ordeyned that he or they the which hath be resceyved or shalbe resseyved here aftir into a brothir of the same Fraternite if it so hadde be that he or they have ben or hadde ben of the Craft of Glovers of the forseid Cite of London paieth or dooth to paie everych of hem for his in comynges xl d. or elles as the Maistres Kepers or Wardeyns of the Fraternite aforeseid and othir iij. brethren of the same Craft and Fraternite to gedir mow accorde. And also it is ordeyned that he and they that so have ben resceyved or have ben resceyved into a brother or a brotherhood of the same Fraternite and everych of hem shal be sworen on the boke so helpe hem God and Holydom that he and they well and truly shal kepen holden and fulfille in alle the ordynnances and articles of the same Fraternite of the Craft of Glovers of the forseid Cite of London kepyng upon the peynes in the ordynances and articles aforeseid above specified.

Also it is ordeyned that the day of the feste that every brothir whenne that they have eten shal go to the forseid Chapell of oure Lady in the Newchurchawe beside London i set personlich to gedir an ther to ben and contynue the tyme of Placebo and Dirige for alle the brethren and sistren of the Fraternite and on the morow aftir atte the oure of viij to be at Masse of Requiem and fro thens to come to gedir to her halle in payne of xvij d. to ben paied in maner and fourme above seid and so that Sonday twellmoth as the yer commeth about to that thanne be mad a quarter day and so the Dirige to be kept yerly in manner and form above said.

Also it is ordeyned that if any of the same Craft or Bretherhood of what degre he be revyle any man of the same Lyverey with any foule langage as thus lying falsyng or sclaunderyng or with any word unlefully violensely and ther be made compleynt to the Wardeyns and therof be atteynt by recorde that thenne anone he be warned by the Clerk of the Craft that he come tofore the Maister and Wardeyns of the Craft therto be examyned and therto make a fyn of vj s. viij d. di. to the olde werk of the Church of Seynt Poule and the othir di. to the box of the same Craft of Glovers.

Also it is ordeyned that alle the Brethren of the same Fraternite the Sonday next folowyng aftir Trinite Sonday to here mete to gedir shull goo and that every brothir of the same Fraternite of the same Craft be warned atte that mete to come by the Maistres Kepers or Wardeyns of the same Fraternite the which for the tyme ben or by her servants other her familiaryes or elles here deputees due tymes and that every brothir and sister paie to his mete xx d. that is to wete for hym self xij d. and his wyfe viij d. and on the morow aftir for hym self iiij d. and thagh his wife come nomore and if more that day be spende falle upon the Maistres for that tyme beyng as the maner is and that the Maistres or Wardeyns the which for the tyme shulbe in the same Sonday in the which afore seid to gedir owen for to etc. and on the morew aftir thenne sewyng without any lette of the resseittes by hem for alle the ij yere afore tofore alle the Brethren of the same Craft shull make a trewe accompt and yelde other elles that they be redy of here accompte with ynne xv daies aftir othir elles that every Maistre Kepers or Wardeyns for the tyme beyng paie for suche defaute eithir of hem in xiij s. iiij d. that is to wete xx d. to the olde werke of the Church of Seynt Poule and the othir xx d. to the box of the same Fraternite.

Also it is ordeyned that no maner person of the Crafte of Glovers presente to fore the Chamburlayn of London no man to make hym free lesse thenne he be presented to fore the Maistres or Wardeyns of the Craft of Glovers upon peyne of vj s. viij d. to be paied xl d. to the Church of Seynt Poule and xld. to the box of the same Craft of Glovers.

Also if any of the same Craft of Glovers be founden contrarying to do ayens the poyntes a fore seid of ayeyns any of hem thanne that he be somoned by the office atte the sute of the Wardeyns of the same Craft for the ffirst defaute he to paie xl d. the on half to be paied to the olde work of the Churche of Seynt Poule and the othir di. to be paied to the box of the same Craft of Glovers and atte the secounde defaute vj s. viij d. and atte the thirde defaute x s. and so forth fro tyme to tyme til he wol obeye to the good rules and ordinaunces of the Craft of Glovers and for to be rered in maner and fourme a fore seid.

Also it is ordeyned if any maner man of the forsaid Craft of Glovers of what degre he be disobeye any rules ordynances or articles lawfully made by the goode avys of the Maistre and Wardeyns that ben for the tyme and othir vj Brethren of the same Craft of Glovers that ben nedeful and profitable for the comen welfare of the seid Craft and also to the gode profite to alle the Kynges lege pepull be not denyed upon the peyne of xiij s. iiij d. that is to sey vj s. viij d. to be paied to the olde werk of the Churche of Seynt Poule of London and vj s. viij d. to the box of the same Craft of Glovers atte the first defaut and atte the secounde defaut ij marcs and atte the iij ^{de} defaut x s. to be rered and paied in maner and fourme above seid.

Also that noon apprentice of the same Craft in the ende of his terme be made freman lasse thenne the Maister and Wardeyns of the seid Craft for the tyme beyng with his Maister or his lawfulle depute presente hym able afore the Chamburlayn and that no man of the seid Crafte selle ne alien the terme of his prentice without the avys and counceille of the Maister and Wardeyns of the seid Crafte for the tyme beyng and that no man of the seid Crafte teche or enfourme any foreyn or straunger in the seid Crafte in hyndryng of the same upon payne of vj s. viij d. as ofte as any be founde defectyf to be paied in maner and fourme above said.

Anno Millesimo ccc^{mo} liiij^{to} et anno regni Regis Edwardi Tercii post Conquestum xxviij^{o} per ordinancionem fratrum subscriptorum.

Qui quidem Fratres de Arte Cirothec' videlicet:

Symon Spenser	Petrus Haberdassher
Willielmus Derby	Johannes Roger
Willielmus de Pilton	Willielmus Sprygge
Johannes de Cornewaille	Robertus Martyn, White Tawier
Ricardus de Banbury	Thomas Crowcher
Johannes Grundhill	Walterus Gosgrove
Johannes Elmestow	Johannes Yaneslee
Johannes Coke	Johannes White
Symon Haverhille	Stephanus le Burner
Robertus de Preston	Johannes Derneford
Adarnus de Thurston	Walterus de Bedelle
Galfridus de Salisbury	Willielmus de Burton
Johannes Guygge	Willielmus Bisshop
Petrus de Preston	Robertus de Chesterfeld
Johannes de Ratford	

Fidem fecerunt bene et fideliter tenere et adimplere omnes ordinaciones antedictas.

Wm. FOX, Registrar.

APPENDIX III

The Case of John Archer 1640

That the glovers of Southwark needed rule and government is illustrated by the case of John Archer. In 1640 the leather workers, many of them based in Southwark, rioted along with the City apprentices in search of the unpopular Archbishop Laud. They marched on Lambeth Palace but their intended victim had escaped. John Archer, a glover, was among those apprehended. He was said to be a ringleader and was tortured on the rack. The State Papers show that on 21 May a warrant was addressed to the Lieutenant of the Tower requiring him to cause Archer to be carried to the rack and there examined on such questions as he, Sir Ralph Whitfield, and Sir Robert Heath 'shall think fit to propose to him; and if, upon sight of the rack, he shall not make a clean answer to the questions, then our further pleasure is that you cause him to be racked as in your discretions shall be thought fit. And when he shall have made a full answer, then the same is to be brought to us and you are still to detain him close prisoner till you shall receive further orders.' The warrant was in the King's hand.[1] It is said that Archer was the last to receive the rack as a means of extorting confession.[2]

---

[1] PRO SPD 16/454/39 No.83. A note in the printed Calendar of State Papers Domestic states 'Copy in the King's own hand although apostilled in Mr. Read's hand, secretary to Secretary Windebank.'

[2] Valerie Pearl, *London and the Outbreak of the Puritan Revolution* (London, 1961), p.107, where she says 'John Archer, a glover of Southwark, said on the flimsiest of evidence to be the ringleader, was brutally tortured before his execution'.

APPENDIX IV

Ordinances of the Glovers' Company made in 1681

ORDINANCES devised and made by the Master Wardens Assistants and Fellowship of the Company of Glovers of the Citty of London for the good Order and Government of the said Company.

Imprimis. That every person or persons that are or shall be members of the said Company whither free or not free of the City and Live in London or Westminster or within three miles of either of them useing or that shall use the trade Art or mistery of a Glover or, any part thereof, shall Submitt be Subject and obedient to the good Government and all the good and wholsome Orders and Ordinances that are or shall be made for the Government of the said Company; And if any such member of the said Company shall breake or not yeild obedience to any of the said Orders or Ordinances he shall have such reasonable mulct or punishment inflicted upon him as the Master Wardens and Court of Assistants of the said Company shall thinke fitt and impose upon him for such his disobedience And that every such Member of the said Company that shalbe minded to take an Apprentice shall after one monthes tryall had of such Apprentice present him to the Master and Wardens of the said Company for the time being, to be by him or them admitted or allowed to be bound. And if any of the said Members of the said Company shall faile or neglect soe to doe he shall pay for such his default to the use of the said Company Five markes towards relief of the poore of the said Company; And further that every one of the said Members haveing any Apprentice soe allowed of and bound with the consent of the Master & wardens, that shall at any time after be minded to Assigne, sett or turne over such apprentice to any other person or persons he shall first present him to the Master and Wardens to the end they may give their consent and approbation thereof; And he that shall faile herein shall forfeit and pay the sume of Forty shillings to the said Company for the use of their poore. And that the names of all the said apprentices that shall be soe turned over shall be entred by the Clerke of the said Company in a booke to be kept for that purpose for which he shall have and receive of the party twelve pence and the Beadle six pence for sumoning them and his attendance upon the Master and Wardens at the doeing thereof.

Item. That every Apprentice to be bound to any Member of the said Company shall be first brought to the Hall of the said Company to be there bound, And his Indenture shalbe made by the Clerke or his deputy for the terme of Seaven Yeares at the least And noe Indenture shalbe made elswhere, for which the Master of such Apprentice shall pay the Company Two shillings and sixpence, And to the Clerke two shillings and to the beadle sixpence; And every M^r offending herein shall forfeit and pay to the use of the Company Fourty shillings. And that noe Journyman of the said Trade shall take any Apprentice untill he hath made proof and given satisfacion to the Master Wardens and Court of Assistants of his being a Sufficient workman, and be by them allowed and admitted to take an apprentice, For which he shall pay xx^s to the use of the Company And two shillings Eight pence to the Clerke and Eight pence to the Beadle, And he that shall presume to Act contrary hereunto shall forfeit & pay for every such offence Five pounds to the use of the Company.

Item that all and every person and persons which now doe or hereafter shall use the said trade of a Glover within the Citty of London or Liberties thereof or within three miles compasse from every side of the said City shall upon Summons given or left to or for them by the Officer of the said Company at the time therein appointed shall appeare before the said Master Wardens & Assistants at their Common Hall or publique place of meeting and there produce before them a good Certificate or sufficient Wittnesses to testifie that he hath served as an Apprentice to that trade the terme of Seaven Yeares And if they allow or approve his Certificate or other testimony therein he shall then be admitted & received a member of the said Company and shall thereupon pay to the use of the Company Twenty Shillings and to the Clerke Two shillings eight pence and to the Beadle Eight pence. And every person useing the said Trade and haveing served thereunto for the terme of Seaven Yeares that shall desire to worke as a Journeyman shall first make like proofe as abovesaid of his Service before the said Master and Wardens and then be by them admitted thereunto and his name entered for that purpose by the Clerke; For which he shall pay to the use of the Company Six Shillings Eight Pence and to the Clerke Sixpence And to the Beadle three pence, And every Journyman offending herein shall forfeit and pay to the Company for ye use of their poore Twenty Shillings:

Item that the Master and Wardens upon Complaint to them made by any member of the said Company against his Apprentice Journiman or Covenant Servant, shall send for the servant or servants complained of and

Examine Order and determine the matter betweene the Master & Servant as the case in reason and Equity shall require; And if any Master shall in such case refuse to subject to and observe what shall be soe Ordered by the said Master and Wardens he shall forfeit and pay to the use of the Company Twenty shilling, And every Journyman not conforming thereto shall forfeit tenn shillings, And Apprentices that shalbe Stubborne and refractory in such cases shall have due correction Laid on them by order of the said Master and Wardens as is usuall in other Companies:

Item that noe Master being a member of the said Company and useing the trade of a Glover shall keepe in his Service to work or imploy in the said trade as a Journiman or otherwise any person comeing out of the Countrey who is or shall not be free of the said Company or bound to him as an Apprentice unless he be first presented to the Master and Wardens at the next Court Day And produce a good Certificate before them of his Lawfull Service to the said trade for the terme of 7 yeares, And be by them Allowed of and Admitted: For which he shall pay to the use of the said Company the Sume of Six Shillings and Eight pence And to the Clerke Sixpence and to the Beadle three pence And every Master offending herein shall forfeit and pay to the use of the Company the Sume of Forty shillings:

Item that noe Journiman to any Member of the said Company useing the said trade shall depart his Masters Service without a months warning given to the Master: Nor any Master being a Member of the said Company shall entertaine any other members Journiman without his former Masters consent Signified by a Certificate under his hand; And alsoe that no Master shall turne away his Journiman without giveing him a fortnights warning upon paine that every Master offending in either of theis perticulers shall for every offence forfeit and pay the sume of twenty Shillings to the use of the Company for reliefe of their poore.

Item that for the better regulation of the said Trade and rule and Governmᵗ of all persons exercising the same within the City of London and three miles Compasse on every side thereof The Master Wardens and Assistants of the said Company of Glovers or any three of them or their Deputies or Assignes in that behalfe from time to time appointed under the Common seale of the said Company shall and may in lawfull manner at all times convenient in any place or places within the said Citty and three miles compasse thereof Search & Examine all manner of Gloves and Glovers ware to be there put to Sale either by wholesale or retaile And see that the same be good and Sufficient both in Leather and Workmanship And for that purpose shall and may Lawfully and peaceably in the day time with a Lawfull Officer enter into all houses shops cellars Warehouses Roomes Inns Osteries and into all other place and places whatsoever within the said City and three miles Compasse thereof where any such wares shall be brought kept and put to sale; And if upon such Search they shall finde any Gloves or Gloversware to be made deceiptfully of Lamb Calf Buck mixed leather or otherwise or Unworkman Like cutt or sewed or of murraine or rotten Leather or unwashed or other insufficient Leather whereby the same will be unserviceable or the buyer or wareer may be thereby abused then all such Gloves and Glovers ware to be taken and brought to the Guild Hall of the Citty of London and if upon a lawfull Enquiry by Jury and tryall according to the Law and Custome in that behalfe they shalbe found defective the said Gloves and Gloversware shalbee destroyed. And every person or persons selling gloves or gloversware whither free of the said City or not who shall oppose or refuse such Search to be made shall for every time offending herein be brought before the Rᵗ Honoᵇˡᵉ the Lord Mayor or some other Justice of the peace within the said City or the Liberties of the said Companyes Charter to be dealt with all according to Law, And alsoe that all and every person and persons Selling Gloves and Gloversware within the Citty of London and Liberties thereof and three miles Compasse of the said City who are not members of the said Company shall pay fower pence quarterly to the said Company of Glovers (as is accustomed in other companies) towards defraying their Charge in mainteining continuall Searchers for the discovery and prevention of Cheats and frauds which might be put upon the people by insufficient and deceiptfull wares.

Item. That every person being a Master that shall exercise the Art or trade of a Glover within the Limitts aforesaid shall pay to the Master Wardens and Assistants their Deputy or Deputies for the use of the said Company Eight pence every Quarter of a Yeare; And every Journyman and Journywoman shall pay fower pence Quarterly which they shall constantly leave in ye hand of their Master that they worke with for the use of the Company, And their said Master shall pay it to the Warden or Wardens of the Company when he or they goe about to gather the said Quarteridge; And the Master of every Journiman or Journywoman that shall refuse to pay the said fower pence quarterly and leave it in their Masters hand as aforesaid that said Master shall discharge him or her from working any longer with him without certificate upon warning given him soe to doe by the Master Wardens and Assistants or some officer of the said Company or other person by their Order And if any Master Glover shall disobey refuse or neglect to observe this order he shall forfeitt and pay for his default herein the sume of Fourty shillings to the said Company for the use of their poore.

Item that if any Controversyes shall arise or unseemly abusive or revileing words shall happen to breake out and be used betweene any members of the said Company the whole matter in difference betweene them shall be referred to and carefully examined by the Master & Wardens of the said Company to be by them

Compromised and agreed before any suite at Law be comenced or prosecuted betweene the said parties, And the person or persons refuseing in such cases to make the said reference and to stand by & abide the determination of the said Master & Wardens shall forfeit and pay tenn shillings to the said Company for the use of their poore. And that every Member of the said Company that shall use any unseemly rude or irreverent words or otherwise misbehave himselfe towards the said Master Wardens or Assistants or any of them shall for every offence forfeit & pay to ye said Company for the use aforesd the summe of Fourty Shillings.

Item if any Member of the said Company after that he shall have been duly called and Elected into the Office either of Master or Warden of the said Company of Glovers shall at any time during his continuance in the said Office absent himselfe in the Countrey or otherwise wave or depart from the Service of his said place without consent, he shall then forfeit and pay to the said Company such fine as is accustomed for the fine of such office.

Item that every person being a member of the said Society and a Freeman of the City of London that shall be duly Elected and Chosen into the Office of Master of the said Company And shall refuse to take the said Office upon him shall forfeit and pay to the use of the said Company for such his refusall the sume of twelve pounds of Lawfull English money And every person being a member of the said Society and free of the said Citty that shall be duly elected a Warden of the said Company and shall refuse to hold the said office shall for such his refusall forfeit and pay to the use of the Company Tenn pounds of lawfull English money; And every one being free of the said Company and City that shall be chosen an Assistant of the sd Company and shall refuse to take upon him & execute the said place shall for such refusall forfeit and pay the sume of Eight pounds to the use of the said Company, and shalbe lyable to be afterwards chosen a Warden and Master of the sd Company; And every person that shall be elected and Chosen a Steward of the said Company being a Member of the said Company (there being fower Yearely to be Chosen by the Master Wardens and Assistants into the office of Stewards, who are to make a Feast or diner with wine musicke and attendants on the Lord Maiors Day as is accustomed by severall other Companies And to receive their Bill of Fare to be provided on such Occation from the said Master Wardens and Assistants); And being soe Chosen shall refuse to take upon him and hold the said Office he shall for his refusall and contempt therein forfeit and pay to the use of the said Company the summe of Tenn pounds of lawfull English money, unless the person chosen to the sd Office of a Steward shall take his Corporall Oath before the Lord Mayor of this Citty for the time being that he is not worth in Cleare Estate One hundred pounds in which case the person that shall take the said Oath shalbe excused for that present Yeare from holding the said office of Steward.

Item if any member of the said Company being warned by the Beadle to appear at ye Companys' hall before the Court of Assistants shall not appeare accordingly; unless he have such lawfull Excuse for his not appearing as the Court of Assistants shall allow he shall forfeit and pay to the Company for the use of their poore the Summe of Five Shillings for every default, And every Assistant of the said Company being warned to any Court of Assistants and not appearing accordingly, he haveing noe just excuse which shall be allowed of by the Court of Assistants, shall for every such default forfeit and pay to the Company for their poore Five Shillings, And whosoever of the Assistants faileth at any time to appeare at the said Court at the hour appointed shall pay to the use of the poore one Shilling, And if any such depart the Court of Assistants without leave first obteined from the said Court he shall pay to the use of the Company for every such default the summe of one Shilling.

Item that all and every person and persons within the City of London and Liberties thereof and within three miles compasse, Widow or Widowes of any Member of the said Company which useth or shall use the trade of a Glover shall upon warning given by the Beadle or otherwise appeare before the Court of Assistants at the Hall of the said Company and there present her Apprentice or Apprentices and be admitted by the said Court, And shall pay for the same to the use of the Company for relief of their poore Ten shillings and to the Clerke one shilling and to the Beadle sixpence.

Item that all & every person and persons within the Citty of London and liberties thereof and within three miles Compass of the said City being now free of or admitted into the said Society of Glovers or which hereafter shallbe made free or admitted into the same shall from time to time according to his or their degree beare his or their part and contribute his or their equall Summe or proportion of money to the Master Wardens and Assistants or the person to be by them thereunto appointed for and towards the paying and defraying of all charges and expences disbursed or to be disbursed about the Comon affaires of the said Company or for the support or well being thereof that shall or may be equally charged upon him or them by the Master Wardens and Assistants or the greater number of them upon paine that every person refusing to contribute and pay any summe so assessed upon him shall forfeit and pay to the use of the said Company the Summe of Forty Shillings.

Item that the Assistants of the said Society of Glovers shall nor exceede the Number of one & twenty, And they shall consist of the Master and Fower Wardens for the time being and Sixteene other Members of the said Company being Freemen of the said Citty who have borne the office of Master or Renter Warden to be chosen according to their degree in the said Company, and when any of the said Number sball happen to Die or be removed for insufficiency or misdemeanour that then the Court of Assistants shall make up and Supply the said Number by choosing in their stead such others of the said Company that have borne either of the said Offices, And every person that shall be chosen and Sworne an Assistant shall upon his admission thereunto pay to the use of the said Company three pounds and to the Clerke two shillings and eight pence for entering his Admission And to the Beadle Eight pence for giveing him notis thereof.

Item that upon the Eight day of September in every Yeare (being the day for Election of the Master and Wardens of the said Company) the person that hath served as Master the Yeare preceding shall (as hath formerly bin accustomed) provide and make a good and handsome Dinner with all things appertaining thereunto at his owne Costs and Charges for the whole Court of Assistants and the officers of the sd Company And if any Master of the said Company shall refuse or faile to provide such Dinner at his goeing out of his Office as aforesaid he shall for his default therein forfeit and pay to the use of the said Company the summe of ten pounds.

Item That the Four Wardens of the said Company shall at their own Costs and Charges Four times in the Yeare vizt upon every Quarter Court day provide a good Dinner for the Court of Assistants as hath formerly bin accustomed; And if the said Wardens shall refuse and faile upon such Court day to make the said Dinner or if any of them shall not beare & pay his part or proportion of the Charge thereof equally with his fellow Wardens, Every Warden makeing default herein Shall forfeit and pay to the use of the said Company for every such default the Summe of Forty Shillings.

Item, that the Master Wardens and Assistants of the said Company of Glovers or the Major parte of them shall and may from time to time soe often and when as they shall thinke Convenient call Choose and admitt into the Livery or Clothing of the said Company such and soe many persons members thereof as they shall thinke meete, the whole number of Liverymen nor exceeding One hundred and twenty at any one time; And that every person soe Elected shall upon his Admission pay therefore to the use of the Company for an towards their meintenance and Support the Sume of Five pounds thirteene shillings and fower pence and to the Clerke of the Company five shillings and to the Beadle two shillings sixpence and shall likewise at his owne proper costs and charges provide himselfe a good Livery Gowne and hood faced with budge according to the Ancient Custome of the Citty and the Constant practice of all other Companies haveing Liveries; And that every person soe Elected into the Livery that shall refuse or deny to take the same upon him or to pay the Severall Sumes aforesd and shall not have just cause or excuse for his said refuseall (as disabled in Estate, that is not being worth one hundred pounds de claro) shall forfeit & pay to the use of the said Company for reliefe of their poore the sume of Ten pounds.

Item that every person Chosen to hold the office of Renter warden shall at his entrance upon the said office enter into Bond to the said Company with two good and Sufficient Securities of the penalty of Two hundred pounds, with Condition that the said Renter-warden shall use and imploy all such moneys plate and other thinges belonging to the said Company which he shall receive or shall come to his hands during the time of his Continuance in the said place in such manner as shall be directed by the Court of Assistants and not otherwise, And that at the Expiration of his Office he shall make and deliver to the Auditors appointed by the said Company at the next Audit Day a true and Just accompt of all the said Moneys plate and other thinges soe by him receaved, and shall after such account made imediatly pay and deliver over what reminder of money or other thinges shall be found in his hands to such person or persons as the Court of Assistants shall appoint, And that upon doeing thereof his Bond shalbe delivered up, And if any person Chosen to the said place of Renter warden shall refuse to give such Security he shall forfeit and pay to the use of the Company for relief of their poore ye sume of Twenty pounds.

Item That the Master and Wardens of the said Company or any of them that shall have any Money goods plate or other things belonging to the Company in their hands shall at the Expiration of their respective Offices bring in to the next Master and Wardens for the Companies use their severall accompts thereof to the end the same may be audited by the persons elected to be the Companies Auditours at their next Audite Day, And that all the just & true accompts of the said Master and Wardens shalbe allowed by the said Auditors and ratified by the next Court of Assistants, And if any Master or Warden shall refuse and faile to make and give such Account and deliver up the Money goods plate &c remaining in his hands he shalbe prosecuted for the same according to Law or forfeit and pay to the use of the Company the summe of tenn pounds.

Item that every person Chosen into the Livery of the said Companie shall at all times when he shall have warning given him by the Beadle of the said Company or other person appointed for that purpose, Appeare at the Hall of the said Company or other place of meeting at the hour appointed in his livery gowne and Hoode, And every one that att such time shall come thither late after the houre appointed sball forfeit one shilling And every one that shall not then appeare at all being within this City the liberties or Subburbs thereof and not disabled by Sickness or other lawfull excuse shall for every default forfeit tenn shillings, And every one that shall depart from the said Hall or other place of Meeting at any of the said times without Leave of the Master and Wardens shall forfeite five shillings All which forfeitures shalbe for the poore of the said Company.

Item that the Master and one Warden shall and may cause any private Court or Courts to be sumoned as occation shall require for the binding of Apprentices or makeing them free when they shall have served their apprenticeships, which private Courts shall Consist of the Master one Wardens & three or four Assistants at ye least.

Item that all and every the Fines Penalties Forfeitures and Sumes of money forfeited or payable by vertue of these ordinances as before is mentioned and expressed and not otherwise herein appointed shall be and goe to the use of the Master Wardens Assistants and Fellowship of the said Company of Glovers to be employed by the Master Wardens and Assistants for the time being in and about the relief of the poore of the said Company and to Susteine and defray the Comon Charge of the said Company And if any person or persons refuse or deny to pay any fine forfeiture Sume or Sumes of Money which by the aforesaid Ordinances or any of them he shall forfeit or ought to pay That then the Master and Wardens of the said Company shall and may cause Suite or Suites to be brought for the same of the Master Wardens Assistants & Fellowship of the said Company in any of his Maties Courts of Records at Westminster or in any of the Courts of record held within the Citty of London by Accion of Debt or Otherwise According to the Lawes of this Realme and the Laudable custom of the said Citty or may distraine for the same at the Eleccon of the said Master and Wardens.

The Oath of the Master

Now that you are Elected and Chosen Master of the Company of Glovers of the Citty of London You shall justly truly and diligently Execute your said Office to the best of your Skill and judgment, You shall to the utmost of your power and soe farr as you lawfully may put in Execution all the Lawful Ordinances made or to be made by Aprobation of the Lord Maior and Court of Aldermen touching the same Company, You shall not punish any person for hatred or Malice or spare any person for reward Dread favour or Affection; And of all and every such goods plate money or other thinges that by reason of your said (office) shall come to your possession or custody You shall make a true and just Accompt to the Court of Assistants or their Deputies Soe helpe you God.

The Oath of the Wardens

Now that you are Elected Warden of the Company of Glovers of the Citty of London You shall Justly truly and Diligently execute your said Office to the best of your skill and judgment You shall be Obedient to the Master and court of Assistants and shall to the utmost of your power and soe farr as you lawfully may put in Execution all the Lawfull Ordinances made or to be made by Aprobation of the Lord Mayor and Court of Aldermen touching the same Company You shall not punish any person for Hatred or malice nor spare any person for reward Dread favour or affection, And of all and every such goods plate money or other thinges that by reason of Your said Office shall come to your possession or Custody You shall make a Just and true accompt to the Court of Assistants or their Deputies Soe helpe you God.

The Oath of every Assistant

Now that you are Chosen an Assistant of the Company of Glovers of the City of London You shall be obedient to and attend the Master and Wardens of the said Company, And to the best of your Skill and knowledge be aiding adviseing and assisting to them in the Affaires and for the Weale and benefit of the said Company; You shall be ready to come to all their Lawfull meetings upon warning given you by the Beadle or otherwise from the said Master and Wardens (except you have a reasonable Excuse) You shall to the best of your power and as farr as you lawfully may observe and keepe and cause to be observed and kept all the Lawfull Ordinances made and to be made for the good government of the said Company according to the true intent and meaning thereof You shall not be of Councell nor aiding nor assisting nor abetting nor reveal any the Secretts of the said Company to any person or persons that are or shall be disobedient refractory or enemies to the said Company, And alsoe all the Lawfull Secretts and Councells of the said Master and Wardens and your fellow Assistants which shall be debated at any the Courts of Assistants or publique meetings for the affaires of the said Company you shall keepe secrett and nor disclose the same out of Court or otherwise to any person or persons whatsoever especially to such whom the same shall or may in any waies touch or concerne Except to the Lord Maior and Court of Aldermen when thereunto required, Soe helpe you God.

The Oath of every Freeman

You shall Sweare to be true to our Soveraigne Lord the King his Lawfull Heires and Successors, You shall be obedient to the Master and Wardens of the Company of Glovers of the City of London for the time being And you shalbe ready to come to all Lawfull meetings upon Warning given to you by the Beadle or otherwise in the behalfe of the said Master and Wardens (Except you have a reasonable Excuse) You shall observe and keepe all the Lawfull Orders & Ordinances made and hereafter to be made for the government and Just guiding of the same Company, You shall likewise keepe all the Lawfull Secretts of the said Company And all such thinges as by way of Councell shall be communicated at any time or times of Assembly by the Master Wardens and Assistants of the said Company at the Hall or place of Meeting for the Affaires of the said Company and not disclose the same to any person or persons whom the same matter may or doth in any wise concerne or touch Except to the Lord Maior and Court of Aldren when required Soe helpe you God.

The Oath of every Liveryman
Now that you are elected and Chosen a Liveriman of the Company of Glovers of the Citty of London You shall Sweare to be true to our Soveraigne Lord the King his lawfull Heires and Successors, You shall be Obedient to the said Master Wardens and Assistants of the said Company for the time being, You shall be ready to come and Attend the Master Wardens and Assistants at the Hall or place of Meeting with your Liverie Gowne and hood upon every warning given by the Beadle or otherwise in the behalfe of the Master Warden and Assistants and not depart License first had and obtained from them, You shall be Obedient to All the Lawfull Ordinances made and hereafter to be made for the Goverment and just guiding of the said Company, Soe helpe you God.

The Clerkes Oath
Now that you are Chosen Clerke to the Master Wardens Assistants and Fellowship of the Company of Glovers of the City of London, You shall Sweare to be true to our Sovereigne Lord the King his Lawfull Heires and Successors, You shall be obedient to the said Master Wardens and Assistants of the said Company when & as offten as they shall require You for the bussiness of Your place as their Clerke, And shall make true entries of all thinges belonging to your Office and committed to your charge without partiality for favour of Affeccion, Lucre, gaine, hatred or Mallice, You shall not wittingly or willingly comitt or doe any thinge to the prejudice hurt or damage of the said Master Wardens Assistants and fellowship of the Company of glovers, But well and truly you shall Execute the said Office of Clerke soe neere as you can, as a good & faithfull clerke ought to doe Soe helpe you God.

The Beadles Oath
Now that you are Elected and Chosen Beadle to the Master Wardens Assistants and Fellowship of the Company of Glovers of the City of London, You shall Sweare to be true to our Sovereigne Lord the King his Lawfull Heires and Successors, You shall soe long as you continue their Beadle Sumon all and every such person and persons as the said Master or Wardens or any of them at any time shall comand to be Sumoned according to the Ordinances of the said Company in that case made or to be made without sparing any person for favour affeccion lucre gaine hatred or malice, You shall indeavour your selfe as neere as you can to doe and Execute all the Lawfull Comandements of the said Mr Wardens and Assistants of the said Company of Glovers and that at all times, And doe all other thinges belonging to your Office which you shalbe Lawfully comanded, You shall not wittingly or willingly committ or doe any thinge to the prejudice damage hurt or rebuke of the said Master Wardens Assistants or Fellowship of the Company of Glovers of the Citty of London, But will truely and diligently you shall Execute your office soe neere as you can as a good Beadle ought to doe, Soe helpe you God.

The Oath of every Journyman
You shall Sweare to be true to our Sovereigne Lord the King his Lawfull Heires and Successors, You shall in all matters be obedient to the Master Wardens & Assistants of the Company of Glovers of the Citty of London and to the good Orders and Ordinances made and to be made for or concerning the said Company. You shall not inbeazell steale wast or consume any Silke leather or any other the Goods of any Master Worke master of the Company aforesaid but behave yourselfe as a true Just and honest Journyman ought to doe to your Master and his family that you worke with Soe helpe you God.

APPENDIX V

The Complaint of John Churchill and others 1700

The cause of Complaint of Mr. John Churchill, Mr. Richard Martyn and severall other of the Assistants of the Company of Glovers London against Mr. Isaac Shard Master of the same Company humbly presented and thus delivered to the Right Honourable the Lord Mayor and Court of Aldermen in Obedience to an Order of the same Court upon the Motion of Mr. Cooper Counsel for the said Master.

That whereas at the time of the comeing on of most of them the said Complainants on the Court of Assistants of the said Company divers disorderly fraudulent and Oppressive Practices were by them Observed to be used and Carryed on therein, to the Dishonour and prejudice of the City as well as to the scandall and detriment of the same Company.

That upon the Choice of John Wildman Clerke January 1693 they the said Complainants more narrowly inspected into the same Abuses.

That thereupon it appeared that some illmen amongst them, from Sinister Designes of their Owne had wittingly and deceiptfully misled the said Company.

That for the Carrying on of the said evill Designes and practices Courts of Assistants were frequently called at Coffee houses Ale houses or Tavernes and private Meetings almost dayly procured on pretence of ye Company's business at such places as aforesaid.

That hereby the Companies Records, Bookes & writings were exposed scattered and lost and not entered kept and preserved as they ought.

That by meanes hereof irregular and fraudulent Bindings and Freedomes were promoted Transacted and Countenanced and Non-Apprentices (in fact) as well as Forreigners and their Apprentices made Freemen of the City contrary to the Antient Customes Liberties and Priviledges of the said City.

The Assistants were needlessly Fatigud and prejudiced.

The Members in Generall unjustly and scandalously Harrassed perplexed and Oppressed.

Severall hereby vitiated and themselves and Families greatly Injured.

The Company's Stock and Income not only extravagantly and unaccountably Impaired and Wasted; But all or great part of the Companies Quarteridge and other theise Branches of their Income fraudulently given and granted to them the same Corrupt Members or some of them or to their Confederates, or negligently permitted to be by them received and applyed to their owne private use and advantage.

That hereby the Company was lessened Impoverished and rendered Weake and contemptible and the City itselfe greatly prejudiced.

That for these Causes the Court of Assistants in the beginning of the yeare 1694 called to accompt the then Master Mr. Joseph Shutt and Renter Warden Mr. John Cave and finding their Management and accounts to be irregular extravagant and scandalous and that the said then Master was no Freeman of London they removed them together with one John Hughes an Assistant for other like sufficient reasons.

That the severall Orders for restraining and preventing these irregularities and exorbitances and especially that of private and frequent Courts made September the 26th 1692 and April 2nd 1694 were by the said designeing Members broken and rendered uselesse and insignificant.

Therefore the Court of Assistants January 14th 1694 (Mr. Farding Master) Ordered that the Master and Wardens and such Assistants as they should choose, should amongst other things, consider of some effectuall wayes to prevent private Corts & Meetings.

That the said then Master and Wardens and such Assistants as they appointed thereto, did, after near Three

Moneths strict Applicacon and Consideracon of the matters aforesaid make their report at their Hall in a full Quarter Court of Assistants Aprill 1st 1695 and then and there it was with unanimous Consent (amongst other things) Agreed and Ordered That no Courts should be held but on the First Monday in every Moneth at the Hall. (Except upon precept from this Honourable Court) And that for as much as the holding of any other Courts was by long experience found to be highly disadvantagious to the Company, expensive to their stock, and detrimentall and injurious to all the Members of the Company, as is thereby declared, Therefore, for remedy thereof and more certaine preventing any other then such Monthly Courts It was further Agreed and Ordered That for any Master Warden or Assistant to act contrary thereto, should be a valid reason for his and their removall, and should cause the Forfeiture of their places and Assistantshipp. It was also then Ordered that the Clerk should have the Custody of the Company's Bookes and papers for the Company's use, to whom the same Court gave power to call for in, and at all times to receive the same.

That hereupon the Company's affaires were more orderly peaceably reputably and successfully managed, and so far was it from bringing any apparent Loss or detriment to the Company that it tended much to their advantage.

That the Corrupt Members not brooking restraint, clamourously complaine of the loss the Company sustained for want of frequent Courts, and Mr. Hobday an ill wisher to the said Orders, being then Master, they thereby obtaine an Order January the 4th 1696, that the Master and Wardens shall have Liberty to make free any persons upon a Necessity, the Company being freed from all Charges therefore.

That, hereby the said Mr. Hobday in the Yeare of his Mastershipp and his Renter Warden Mr. Seall and Mr. Robert Jones who succeeded as Master in the Yeare 1698 and his Renter Warden Mr. John Rowberry and Mr. Henry Collier Rentor Warden in the following yeare 1699 with other Corrupt Members, designed and Endevoured to Elude and pervert the said former Orders, and under Umbrage of the last Order multiplyed their private Courts to the Losse prejudice and disgrace of the Company and that it might not be discerned how the Companys Incombe was misapplyed and by them most profusely and extravagantly spent and consumed they at the End of their respective Yeares, after bringing to account their necessary charges, cause their Accounts to be Modelled by Mr. Brookes or some other of their Confederates and their otherwise unaccountable Expences to be Lumpt at very considerable Sumes and in confederacy with some of the Antients of the said Company refuse to give or render to the Court of Assistants as well ye particular Account of their Receipts [as] of a great number of Fines and other moneys which they or some of them have unduly taken, and of whom, for what, and when the same was received, as also of their Disbursements and Expences in contempt of and contrary to the antient Custome and express Orders of the said Company.

And that whereas John Wildman the Clerke of the said Company had as we humbly conceive, during all this time, endeavoured, faithfully to discharge his said Office and to the best of his Judgment advised to what was regular lawfull and commendable and avoided all he could Countenancing or acting in the said fraudulent and corrupt Designes and practices, the Corrupt Members therefore dislike him and constantly Clamour against him, as too nice and scrupulous & as an Enemy to and Obstructor of the Company's Business and declare they can never be well till he be amoved, and refuse to imploy him in sundry of the most important affaires of the Company whilest they from time to time make use of Mr. Smelt and Mr. Brocket two of the Confederates, in the management and Dispatch of severall Matters of concerne relateing to the Office of ye Clerke, not only to the prejudice of the said Clerke, but disservice of the said Company altho' the major part of the Assistants disapproved thereof, and well liked of his the said Wildman's performance of his Duty in the said place.

And whereas matters thus standing at the time of the choice of the said Mr. Shard Master September 1699 It was reasonably and justly expected that he would have required and caused the aforenamed Masters & Rentor Wardens according to the antient Custome of the said Company & orders of the Court of Assistants to have brought in the particulars of their said receipts transactions & expences to the Court of Assistants that the same might have been known & enterered in the said Company's Bookes as need was, as well for the regular & due keeping of the same Bookes as otherwaies as also that he the said Master would have duely & faithfully according to his place and oath executed & observed the said wholesome Orders or have caused or permitted others to be made to Corroborate the same the better to fence against the said abuses, and the rather for that hetherto he alwaies seemed Zealous in detecting and opposing the said abuses & passing such accounts as aforesaid & that he would have observed the necessary and antient Custome & direct Ordinances of the Company in causing the present Rentor Warden Mr. Copeland to give security for the Company's Effects comeing to his hands and have permitted him to receive the moneys of the said Company and that the said Master would in these and all other things have observed maintained & kept the antient Customes and knowne Constitutions of the said Company & thereby preserved the peace, & sought the prosperity & welfare of the said Company But so it is may it please Your Lordshipp & this honourable Court That the said Mr. Isaac Shard soon after he came into the said Office of Master declared that he would not be restrained or limitted by any orders they had or should make, that he would call Courts as oft' as he should please & would act as he list that he would arrest & sue sundry of the Assistants Livery and others & specially ye Company's Stock to performe his will; Accordingly he unduely getts into his hands the sum of Fifty pounds principall moneys or some other sum or summes belonging to the Company that had been placed out at Interest & which according to the said Company's By:laws & Orders should have been either paid to the said Rentor Warden, Copeland, who ought to give security therefore, or placed out againe at Interest & secretly takes away from the Hall the abstract of the Company's Charter & Ordinances & detaines the same tho' the same was made and requested to be ready for the use of the Court of Assistants, he also requires of the Clerke the Company's Bookes & papers who pleading the aforesaid Order for his having the custody of them & desireing the Direcion of the Court of Assistants therein he the said Master thereupon violently & contrary to the good likeing of the Court of Assistants, seizes and takes from him severall of the said Bookes, & in further Violation of his the said Master's Oath & in breach of the By:laws Orders and Constitucons of the said Company he summonses a Court, other than on the Monethly Day, & violently then forces the question to have the same, allowed of & to have all the said former Orders repealed And tho' the Major part of the Court of Assistants then protested against the same & caused the same to be Entered; Yet the said Master having about 5 that joyned with him therein by Menaces & otherwise attempts to force the Clerke to enter the same as an Order of Court & at other times attempts to act and make Orders of Court by about one third of the Assistants and altho' the Court of Assistants on the next Monthly Court Day confirmed their said former Orders made Aprill lst 1695 & when he the said Master pretended a need of frequent Courts to prevent any Parliamentary Duty on Leather the Court of Assistants offered to give him power therefore, yet he not contented therewith maliciously pursueing the full breach of the same Orders & resolvedly and unweariedly endeavouring to lay the said Company open to all the Enormities & pernicious practices that were heretofore practiced calling in & takeing to his assistance the said Corrupt Members, did on or about the sixth day of May last irregularly violently & unduely attempt the repealing of the same, and falsly & unjustly asserts that he or they have so done And agreeably thereto he the said Master declared that he would have no Monethly Courts, altho' the same hath been the antient & constant practice of the said Company & accordingly wilfully & resolvedly omitts & refuses to summons Courts on the proper stated & accustomed Daies but calls them at other times when most of the Members of the said Company conceived themselves not obliged to attend, and at same such Court or Courts so irregularly unduely & fraudulently held & managed falsly & unjustly pretended to have repealed, or confirmed the repeale of the said Orders, & also to have discarded the said Clerke without any accusation by, or hearing in, the Court of Assistants & to have some Order or Orders to have the Bookes Committed to him, & in default, by Law to enforce the Clerke thereto, & refuses to give any due proofe, or proper Testimony that the same pretended Order or Orders of his were the regular, free, certaine & express Order or Orders of the said Court of Assistants And contrary to his Duty & Oath as a Citizen did refuse the Clerkes appeale to this Honourable Court but exhibitts a Bill in the high Court of Chancery against him & creates frequent Meetings, & thereby needlessly consumes the Company's Stock & without the knowledge & approbation of the Court of Assistants causes one Mr. East to Officiate as Clerke, & irregularly makes him privy to the Affaires of the said Company, & seeks to force him into the said Company as their Clerke And when on the First of July last past a full Court of Assistants mett at their Hall according to their owne Orders and the said Master's Summons he the said Master contrary to their repeated requests & declared good likeing, refused to permitt the said John Wildman to Officiate his place, but required him to withdraw from thence which many of the Assistants then present refuseing to permitt he the said Master & his Accomplices did thereupon Ruffle & Assault some of the Assistants then present & did also thrice maliciously and violently assault him the said John Wildman to the hazzard of his Life, for which said Ryott & assault on the said John Wildman the said Complainants are informed the Grand Jury have found a Bill of Indictment against him the said Master & the said Collier & Rowberry & he the said Master did also dureing all the space the Assistants were there attending which was about 5 hours refuse to act as Master or to put the question whether the said Wildman should withdraw or not, or to put any other of the many questions then Offered or to proceed on any business tho' frequently & respectfully solicited thereto, to the great prejudice Loss & disgrace of the Company; he the said Master & his Adherents did then also as well as before refuse to referr the matters in Difference to this honourable Court altho' the major part of the 29 Assistants then present desired the same & that many of them then present, did draw up and signe a protest against his said proceedings And with these and many other Corrupt, disorderly, arbitrary and unlawfull practices in & concerneing the said Company the said Complainants humbly Conceive the said Master & his adherents, namely, Mr. Christopher Smelt, Mr. Walter Thomas, Mr. Richard Gibson, Mr. John Burch, Mr. Thomas Brookes, Mr. Robert Jones, Mr. William Hobday, Mr. Phillipp Seale, Mr. John Roberry & Mr. Henry Collier, & some others of the Company to be justly chargeable and lyable to the Forfeiture of their Honours, Offices & Places, & all those Franchises & priviledges which in common with other Citizens they were intituled to; And the same Charge, with the leave of this honourable Court are ready to make good.

APPENDIX VI

The Hall of the Glovers' Company

The charter of 1638 empowered the Glovers' Company to 'buy one or more houses to be used as a hall of a value not exceeding the clear yearly value of £40 the statute of mortmain[1] or any other statute notwithstanding'. It went on to give the Company wide powers to buy land either freehold or leasehold and to let or assign it or 'do all other acts or things touching such land'. Land, of course, includes buildings.

Whether the Company proceeded to obtain a hall immediately is not known. Perhaps the unrest and uncertainty of the times followed by the Civil War made them postpone the idea. At all events the Company had a hall by 1675[2] when the earliest minutes of the Courts of Assistants commence.

The Glovers' Hall formerly stood in a Court known appropriately as Glovers' Hall Court, situate off Beech Lane in the Ward of Cripplegate. By 1840, by which time the Hall had long since ceased to be used by the Company, Glovers' Hall Court had become known as Braimes Buildings.

The Hall is shown both on Ogilby and Morgan's map of London dated 1676[3] and on John Rocque's Plan of London, Westminster and Southwark dated 1746.[4] It is in the area bounded by Beech Lane on the North, White Cross Street on the East and Red Cross Street on the West. Looking at Ogilby's map the Court is shown at 'b75' and the Hall itself, seeming impressively large, is marked 'A.20'. The later plan is very informative showing a number of livery halls and Glovers Hall Court is just visible above the figure '18'.

In 1922 Sir John Baddeley, Lord Mayor of London in 1921, published a history of Cripplegate Ward.[5] In it he says that it has been suggested that Glovers Hall was originally a private chapel belonging to the palace of the Abbots of Ramsey and that it came into the possession of Sir Drew Drewrie about 1600 and was then called Drewrie House. It is referred to in the Churchwarden's accounts of St. Giles Cripplegate for 1664-5 when 'the bell ringers paid 3ˢ 6ᵈ when the King came to Glovers Hall'. Prince Rupert was living nearby in Beech Lane and this may have led the King (Charles II) to visit the Hall.

As early as 1662 the building began to be used for religious purposes. Many of the livery halls in the ward were then used as meeting houses by the Nonconformists.[6] Perhaps the fact that Glovers Hall Court was reached by a narrow passageway and hidden from the sight of passersby, effectively giving privacy, meant that the Hall was more attractive to Nonconformists in the 17th and 18th centuries.

Sir John says that on 25 May 1662 a religious service in the Hall was stopped by soldiers; that an ensign entered with sword drawn holding it over the head of the minister before dragging him to Newgate prison. In 1669 the Hall came into the hands of the Baptists who had the largest conventicle or meeting place in the Ward. The Baptists continued there until 1702 after which the premises were used by several denominations.

At the end of the 17th century the Hall was used as a school. In the minute and account book of the Cripplegate Schools Foundation it is recorded that in 1698 a school for 100 boys was opened in White Cross Street. It removed from there to Glovers Hall and afterwards to Barbican.

By 1739 the Wesleyans were using the building. There are several references in John Wesley's Journal to his preaching in Beech Lane.[7] On 13 January 1739 he says he preached to a large company in Beech Lane. In a letter to the Reverend George Whitfield dated 26 February in the same year he wrote 'On Saturday sennight[8] … at Beech Lane where I expound usually to five or six hundred before I go to Mr Exall's society …'. After 1739 there seem to be no further references to Beech Lane until 11 December 1762 when he describes a meeting there as being like 'a bear garden'. Those who prayed 'were partly the occasion of this by their horrid screaming and unscriptural enthusiastic expressions'. Wesley seems to have been appalled. His Journal shows that he removed the meeting to the Foundry[9] and so cured the screaming and delivered the society from worthless members.

---

[1] See Ch. XIV note 14.   [2] And presumably when the King visited it ten years earlier. See post.
[3] See Endpapers.   [4] See page 52.
[5] Sir John James Baddeley, *Cripplegate, one of the Twenty Six Wards in the City of London* (London, 1922). Most of the information in this Appendix is derived from Sir John's book.
[6] Sir John mentions the halls of the Curriers, the Lorriners, the Plaisterers and the Haberdashers as being so used.
[7] None of the references specify Glovers' Hall or Glovers' Hall Court but both Sir John Baddeley and Caroline Gordon and Wilfrid Dewhirst, authors of the more recent *The Ward of Cripplegate in the City of London* (London, 1985) declare that Wesley preached in the Hall.   [8] A week, i.e., a week ago.
[9] A foundry almost opposite Glovers' Hall is mentioned in rate books at the end of the 18th century and doubtless is the place referred to by Wesley.

Whether the Hall was used by any religious group in the next 30 years is not known but in 1793 the Baptist-Sandemanians are said to have leased the Hall for eight years.

Sir John quotes Hughson writing in 1806 as saying 'Glovers Hall which, having been long deserted by the Company, was converted to other purposes.' Another writer, Lambert, a few years later is quoted as saying 'It is a very old building and has been deserted by the Company who now transact their business at the George and Vulture tavern, Lombard Street'.

In 1880 it was rated at £10 and still dignified as 'the Hall'. When Sir John wrote his history in 1922 he says that the northern and eastern walls could still be seen.

APPENDIX VII

Death of Wilfrid Ernest Palmer MBE, MA, MSc
Master of the Worshipful Company of Glovers of London 1961/62

If you check the records of a Livery Company, you will usually be able to find that in the year 1761/62, or whatever year is of interest to you, the Master was XYZ Esq. But in relation to him as a man – absolutely nothing. If the Minutes of Meetings of the Court have been preserved, you may glean a very little from the activities of various individuals, but in the main the pictorial canvas will remain blank.

It is with this thought in mind that I am recording, to be placed if thought fit with the Minutes of the Court Meetings, an account of a most melancholy event which is almost certainly unique in the history of the Livery Companies of the City of London, and almost certainly will never in history occur again.

I refer to the death of our Master in his full regalia in St Paul's Cathedral on Friday, 23rd March, 1962, while waiting with other Masters to receive the Lord Mayor and Sheriffs attending the annual United Guilds service.

Wilfrid Ernest Palmer was born at Great Yarmouth, Norfolk, on 22nd May, 1894. He was educated at Bishops Stortford and St John's College, Cambridge, where he was a Foundation Scholar and Prizeman (MA). He was also Le Blanc Medalist (MSc) at Leeds University.

In the First World War (1914/18) he served in the 19th Royal Fusiliers from which he was comissioned to the Dorset Regiment. He saw service in Mesopotamia and was twice mentioned in despatches. In the Second World War, being too old for Army service, he was Divisional Air Raid Warden for Yeovil. It may interest the future readers of this memoranda to know that the population of Yeovil was then approximately 24,000.

He retired from active commercial life in 1953 and was then Chairman and Managing Director of Whitby Brothers Ltd., glove manufacturers of Yeovil. He was a Past President of the National Association of Glove Manufacturers. It would be difficult to think of a man more fitted to be Master of our Worshipful Company.

He was clean shaven, baldish, of slim, neat build, rather precise in his manner, and very intelligent. He was always most courteous, polite, kind, friendly and considerate of others, and regarded by his brethren on the Court with esteem and affection. During his short period as Master, he handled the affairs of the Company with a high degree of competence.

On Friday, 23rd March, 1962, at noon, the United Guilds Service was held at St Paul's Cathedral, the Service being taken by the Right Reverend and Right Honourable R. W. Stopford, CBE, DD, DCl, the Bishop of London.

I arrived in the Cathedral at about 11.30 a.m. and robed. I spoke to a friend for a minute or two, and when I returned I found the Master robing. He had on his gown and the assistant Beadle was helping him with the Chain of Office. It was twisted at first, taken off, and put back properly.

When this was done, I spoke to the Master, and he thanked me for coming to the service and supporting him, a courteous gesture and typical of the man. We then went to Pew 31 which was reserved for our Company, and we were later joined by Past Master Pinkham and various Members of the Livery.

The formal procession as set out in the Programe of the Service was as follows:

A Virger

The Choir

The College of Minor Canons

A Virger

The Beadles of the Grocers' and Mercers' Companies

The Masters or Prime Wardens of the Companies of

Grocers	Mercers
Fishmongers	Drapers
Merchant Taylors	Goldsmiths
Haberdashers	Skinners
Ironmongers	Salters
Clothworkers	Vintners
Glovers	Clockmakers

Framework Knitters	Felt Makers
Gardeners	Needle Makers
Wheelwrights	Tin Plate Workers
Patten Makers	Distillers
Coach and Coach Harness Makers	Glass Sellers

The Chairman of the Committee
A Virger
The Marshal
High Officers
The Sheriffs
The Court of Aldermen
The Dean's Virger
The Receiver and Registrar
(Master of the Scriveners' Company)
The Bishop's Chaplain bearing the Crozier
The Lord Bishop
Supported by
The Dean and Chapter
The Lord Mayor's Chaplain

The Sergeant at Arms   The Sword Bearer

The Right Honourable the Lord Mayor

At about 11.50 the Master told me that he was proceeding to the assembly point and asked me to keep an eye open for him as he approached and make sure he did not pass our pew. I joked with him as to the means I would use to attract his attention. We both laughed and with a friendly wave of the hand he left, proceeding towards the beginning of the aisle. He appeared to be perfectly happy, and in good health. It was the last time any Member of the Company saw him alive. Within a minute or so he was dead.

People, I know not whom – came to the pew to tell us that our Master had collapsed, and that it was serious. I hurried with Past Master Pinkham to the western end of the Cathedral. Our Master's body was lying on the floor of the Cathedral, and it was clear at a glance that he was dead. He was still wearing his gown, but the Chain of Office had been removed and his collar and tie loosened.

The Master of another Company told me that our Master was about to take his place in the procession when he fell like a stone. My informant added that it appeared that death was instantaneous and he was dead before he struck the ground.

A doctor who was present examined him before we arrived and stated there was nothing he could do for him, and an ambulance was sent for by the Police.

We were too stunned to do anything but express our horror at what had occurred. I was asked if I would join the procession in place of the Master but declined. We were joined a moment or two later by Senior Warden West (who also declined), Past Master Thomas, and the Clerk of the Company, Mr. H. M. Collinson. We stood between the Master's body and the public to screen it from view as much as possible until the ambulance arrived.

It must be unique for the Master of a Livery Company to lie dead in his regalia in St Paul's Cathedral in the presence of the Bishop of London, the Lord Mayor of London, the Sheriffs, a host of civic dignitaries, the Masters of all the other Companies, and a concourse of Past Masters, Wardens and liverymen.

I record this event in deep sorrow, impelled solely by a sense of history, and with a feeling that this record may be of interest to those as yet unborn, and who may read this when we are all dead and forgotten.

(signed) Victor Morley Lawson

Third Under Warden 1961/62

APPENDIX VIII

The Masters of the Company

1638-9	William Smarte	1800-1	Joseph Hibbert
1639-75	Records missing	1801-2	Joseph Butterworth
1675-6	Francis Aldwyn	1802-3	Robert Taylor
1676-7	Richard Read	1803-4	Luke Flood
1677-8	Robert Jones	1804-5	Josiah Monnery
1678-9	Humphrey Griffith	1805-66	Records missing
1679-80	William Webb	1866-7	T. Clarke
1680-1	Thomas Brooks	1867-8	Robert Alexander Gray
1681-2	Richard Gibson	1868-9	Charles James Jones
1682-7	Records missing	1869-70	George Hibbert
1687-8	Edmond Farding	1870-1	Robert Alexander Gray
1688-92	Records missing	1871-2	Edward Hibbert
1692-3	William Rutter	1872-3	George Hibbert
1693-4	Joseph Shutt	1873-4	Edward Hibbert
1694-5	Edmond Farding	1874-5	George Hibbert
1695-6	Daniel Wharley	1875-6	Edward Hibbert
1696-7	William Hobday	1876-86	George Hibbert
1697-8	Robert Jones	1886-9	Henry Homewood Crawford
1698-9	Records missing	1889-90	Charles John Shoppee
1699-1700	Isaac Shard	1890-1	Charles George Hale
1700-72	Records missing	1891-2	Albert Joseph Altman
1772-3	John Kentish	1892-3	John Charles Bell
1773-4	James Piercy	1893-4	Lt. Col. George Lambert
1774-5	John Pollard	1894-5	Frederick C.D. Haggard
1775-6	William Frampton	1895-7	Major John Roper Parkington JP
1776-7	Josiah Monnery		FRGS
1777-8	William Parry	1897-8	Charles Hampton Hale
1778-9	John Burnell	1898-9	Henry Homewood Crawford
1779-80	Robert Lewin	1899-1900	John Charles Bell (Alderman)
1780-1	John Popplewell	1900-1	Charles George Hibbert
1781-2	Richard Draper	1901-2	Arthur Hibbert
1782-3	William Griffiths	1902-3	Col. Sir John Roper Parkington DL
1783-4	Benjamin Robertson		JP FRGS
1784-5	Robert Threlfal	1903-4	Lewis Edmund Glyn KC
1785-6	William Wryghte	1904-5	Sir Ernest Clarke
1786-7	John Hemans	1905-6	Sir Henry Homewood Crawford
1787-8	Timothy Fisher	1906-7	Gilbert Purvis
1788-9	James Devereux Hustler	1907-8	Sir John Charles Bell (Alderman
1789-90	Christopher Parker		and Lord Mayor)
1790-1	Thomas Heathfield	1908-9	Thomas Adolphus Bullock FRGS
1791-2	Daniel Jennings	1909-10	Charles Jones Cuthbertson
1792-3	Richard Ladyman	1910-12	Herbert Charles Marshall
1793-4	William Platell	1912-13	Frank Debenham JP
1794-5	John William Anderson (Alderman)	1913-14	Alfred Mosely CMG
1795-6	John Rowlatt	1914-15	Sir John Roper Parkington DL JP
1796-7	Matthew Stainton		FRGS
1797-8	William Eamonson	1915-16	John Edmund Drower
1798-9	John Pollard	1916-17	James Roll (Alderman)
1799-1800	William Parry	1917-18	Ernest Webb

1918-19	Henry Terrell	1961-2	Wilfrid Ernest Palmer MBE (died in
1919-20	James Morrison McLeod		office Cecil Ernest Donne
1920-1	James Roll (Alderman)		succeeded as Acting Master)
1921-3	Samuel Amos Worskett	1962-3	Alfred William West
1923-4	Thomas H. Openshaw CB CMG	1963-4	Major Sir Reginald Bullin OBE TD
1924-5	George Cockburn Jack		JP
1925-6	Harold Watson Humphries FCA	1964-5	Harold Walker OBE
1926-7	Ernest Frank Donne	1965-6	Victor Morley Lawson
1927-8	Canon Fitzwilliam John Catrer	1966-7	James Birkmyre Rowan TD JP
	Gillmor	1967-8	William Gray Rowan JP
1928-9	Edmund Victor Huxtable	1968-9	Vice-Adm. Sir Charles Hughes
1929-30	Harold Edmund Franck		Hallett KCB CBE
1930-1	William Samuel Green	1969-70	Herbert John Morris
1931-2	Joseph Henry White	1970-1	Vivian Charles Boulton
1932-3	Lionel Ernest Howard Whitby	1971-2	Ernest Albert Copeland
1933-4	Sir Charles Henry Collett	1972-3	Clifford Henry Barclay
	(Alderman and Lord Mayor)	1973-4	Philip David Froomberg
1934-5	Claude Henry Evans	1974-5	Frederick Ivor Richard Marwood
1935-6	Col. Sir George McLaren Brown		Spry
	KBE	1975-6	Eric Vernon Hawtin
1936-7	Alexander Mackenzie Hay	1976-7	Davide Patrick Leith Antill TD
1937-8	Frederick Whittingham JP	1977-8	Leslie Eustace Warner OBE (died
1938-9	George Sherington Collins		in office Clifford Henry Barclay
1939-40	Major Richard Rigg OBE JP		succeeded as Acting Master)
1940-2	Sir Sydney Parkes	1978-9	Henry Renault Beakbane FRSA
1942-3	Austin Leonard Reed	1979-80	William Randolph Spencer
1943-4	William Craven-Ellis MP	1980-1	Barry St George Austin Read CBE
1944-5	Cecil Ernest Donne		MC DL FRSA
1945-6	Estcourt Southcombe OBE (died	1981-2	Ald. Sir Christopher Collett GBE
	in office Frederick Whittingham		FCA
	succeeded as Acting Master)	1982-3	Neville Rayner JP
1946-7	Thomas Brammall Daniel FRIBA	1983-4	Clifford Edwin Adams
1947-8	George William Heard	1984-5	Hans Stephen Kirsch
1948-9	Frederick John Giles	1985-6	Frederick William Caine FCA
1949-50	William Herbert Leslie Pinkham	1986-7	Harold Grenville Walker
1950-1	James George Rowan JP	1987-8	Kenneth David St John Smith
1951-2	Alexander Froomberg		ADipl ARIBA FRSA
1952-3	Norman Loveless	1988-9	Clive William Lidstone MBE FRSA
1953-4	Lt. Col. Lyndall Fownes Urwick	1989-90	John Stanley Bishop
	OBE MC	1990-1	Maurice Sidney Lea FCA FRSA
1954-5	James Ernest Franck FRIBA	1991-2	David Mathieson Anderson CA
1955-6	Major Harold Charles Ernest	1992-3	Charlesworth John Wood FRSA
	Oliver MC JP	1993-4	John Gratwick OBE
1956-7	Albert Henry Shanks	1994-5	John Jotham Gardner FCII
1957-8	Edward Royden Alltree	1995-6	Alan Seymour Fishman FIA ASA
1958-9	Albert John Thomas FRIBA	1996-7	Michael Kennedy Down FCA
1959-60	The Very Revd Harold George	1997-8	Emanuel Silverman
	Michael Clarke	1998-9	Malcolm Olaf Penney FCA
1960-1	William Arthur Phillips	1999-2000	Margaret Mavis Linton

APPENDIX IX

Some Clerks of the Company

1638	Richard Fussell (John Harris to be second clerk and to succeed him)
1678	Mr. Draper appears
1682	William Hetherington appears
1693	John Wildman appears
(1772)-1784	James Roberts
1784-1803	Philip Wyatt Crowther
1803-	John Thomas
(1832)-1866	Mr. R. Thomas appears
1867-88	Frederick R. Thomas
1888-1922	Adam William Burn
	(Mr. Burn was later appointed to the Court and became Third Under Warden)
1923-42	J.J. Edwards
1942-7	Frederick Wills
1947-8	Roland Champness
1948-78	Harold Maurice Collinson
1978-82	Peter Lawson-Clarke, FCIB
1982-4	John Jotham Gardner, FCII
1984-93	Group Captain Douglas George Farley Palmer, OBE
1993-	Monique Magdalen Denise Hood, JP

In the case of James Roberts and R. Thomas the dates in brackets are the dates when their names first occur.

Thomas King appears in 1771 and may well have been the clerk at that time but proof is lacking.

Bibliography

Anon., *Poll of the Liverymen of the City of London* (London, 1710)

Ashton, R., *The City and the Court, 1603-1643* (Cambridge, 1979)

Austin, E., *The Law relating to Apprentices including those bound according to the custom of London* (London, 1890)

Baddeley, Sir J.J., *Cripplegate, one of the Twenty Six Wards of the City of London* (London, 1922)

Beck, S. William, *Glovers, their Annals and Associations* (London, 1883)

Black, W.H., *The History and Antiquities of the Worshipful Company of Leathersellers of the City of London* (London, 1871)

Blackham, Col. Robert J., *London's Livery Companies* (London, n.d.)

Campbell, R., *The London Tradesman* (London, 1747)

Doolittle, I.G., *The City of London and its Livery Companies* (Dorchester, 1982)

Elmes, James, *A Topographical Dictionary of London* (London, 1831)

Gordon, Caroline and Dewhirst, Wilfrid, *The Ward of Cripplegate in the City of London* (Cripplegate Ward Club, 1985)

Harbin, Henry A., *A Dictionary of London* (London, 1918)

Hazlitt, W.C., *The Livery Companies of the City of London* (London, 1892)

Hope, Valerie, *My Lord Mayor* (London, 1989)

Jones, P.E., *The Corporation of London: Its origins, constitution, powers and duties* (Oxford, 1950)

Lang, J., *Pride without Prejudice. The Story of London's Guilds and Livery Companies* (London, 1975)

Lawson-Clarke, Peter, *A Brief History of the Worshipful Company of Glovers of London* (London, 1982)

Masters, Betty R., *The Chamberlain of the City of London 1287-1987* (London, 1988)

Pearl, Valerie, *London and the Outbreak of the Puritan Revolution* (London, 1961)

Rees, J. Aubrey, *The English Tradition. The Heritage of the Venturers* (London, 1934)

Riley, H.T., *Memorials of London and London Life* (London, 1868)

Saunders, Ann (ed.), *The Royal Exchange* (The London Topographical Society, 1997)

Sharpe, R.R., *Calendar of Letter Books of the Corporation of the City of London* (London, 1899-1912)

Smith, Toulmin, *English Gilds* (London, 1892)

Unwin, G., *Industrial Organisation in the Sixteenth and Seventeenth Centuries* (London, 1904)

Unwin, G., *The Gilds and Companies of London* (London, 1908)

Walford, Cornelius, *Gilds: their Origin, Constitution, Objects and later History* (London, 1888)

Wesley, John, *Journal*, vols.4 and 12 (1739 and 1762)

Articles, Manuscripts, etc.

British Library: Lansdowne MS 73, 74, 114, 226; Additional MS 12503 and 12504

Corporation of London Record Office: Journals of Common Council, Repertories of Court of Aldermen, Lord Mayor's Waiting Book, Companies' Box and other Company papers

Cooper, C.R.H., 'The Archives of the City of London Livery Companies and Related Organisations' (Guildhall Library, 1985)

Guildhall Library, Archive of the Glovers' Company, Prowet. MS.

Kahl, W.F., 'The Development of the London Livery Companies. An historical essay and select bibliography' (Boston, Mass, 1960)

Kellet, J.R., *The Economic History Review*, 2nd series, April 1958

Leathersellers' Company, Minute books, 1608-50

Public Record Office: State Papers Domestic; Privy Council Papers

Report by the Royal Commission on Municipal Corporations (England and Wales) London and Southwark; London Companies (Parliamentary papers [cmd 239] 1837 xxv)

Report of the Royal Commission on the City of London Livery Companies (Parliamentary papers [cmd 4073] 1884 xxxix)

Thomson, R., 'Leather manufacture in the post-medieval period with special reference to Northamptonshire' (1981)

Thomson, R., 'Leather manufacture through the Ages' (1983)

Index

compiled by Auriol Griffith-Jones

Page numbers in *italic* refer to the Appendices; those in **bold** refer to illustrations

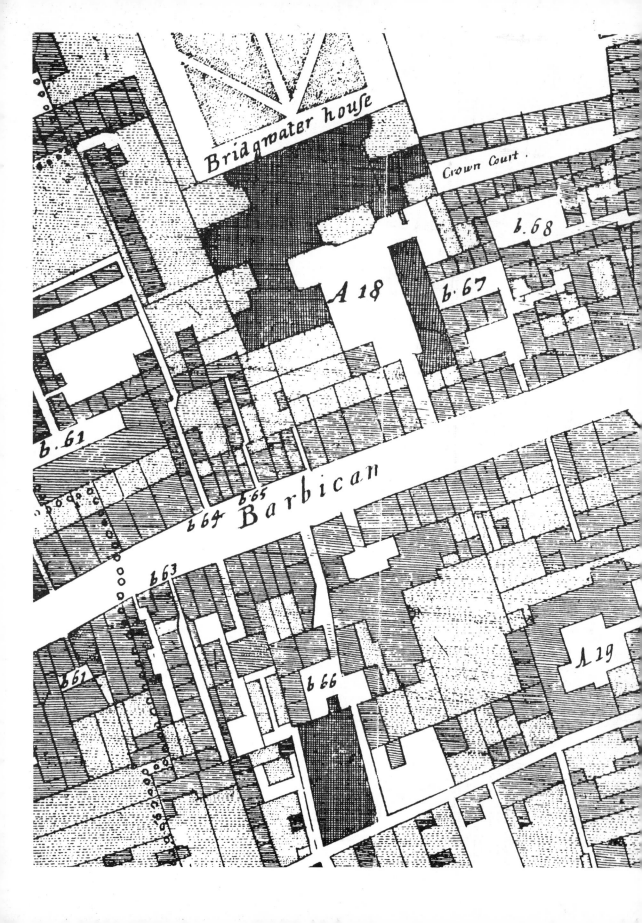

Bridgwater house

Crown Court

b.68

A 18   b.67

b.61

b.64 b.65 Barbican

b.63

b.61

b.66

A 19